10 HABITS
THAT
BLOCK
SUCCESS

DR. PETER BONADIE

10 HABITS THAT BLOCK SUCCESS

Printed in the United States of America

ISBN# 978-0-9991381-7-5 (Paperback)

ISBN# 978-0-9991381-8-2 (Hardcover)

All quotes, unless otherwise noted, are from the HOLY BIBLE, NEW INTERNATIONAL VERSION (NIV). Copyright © 1973, 1978, 1984 by International Bible Society. Used by permission of Zondervan Publishing House. All rights reserved.

Scriptures marked KJV are taken from The Holy Bible, King James Version. Copyright © 1972 by Thomas Nelson Inc., Camden, New Jersey 08103.

Scriptures marked AMP are taken from The Amplified Bible, containing the amplified Old Testament and the Amplified New Testament. 1987. The Lockman Foundation: La Habra, CA.

Scriptures marked AMPC are taken from The Amplified Bible, Classic Edition, Copyright © 1954, 1958, 1962, 1964, 1965, 1987. The Lockman Foundation: La Habra, CA.

Scriptures marked NLT are taken from the New Living Translation of the Holy Bible, copyright © 1996, 2004, 2015 by Tyndale House Foundation, Carol Stream, Illinois 60188. All rights reserved.

Scriptures marked CJB are taken from the Complete Jewish Bible. Copyright © 1998 by David H. Stern. All rights reserved.

Scriptures marked CEV are taken from the Contemporary English Version of the Holy Bible. Copyright © 1995 by American Bible Society. All rights reserved.

Scriptures marked NCV are taken from the New Century Version® of The Holy Bible. Copyright © 2005 by Thomas Nelson, Inc. All rights reserved.

Scriptures marked NET are taken from the New English Translation NET Bible® copyright ©1996-2006 by Biblical Studies Press, L.L.C. http://netbible.com. All rights reserved.

Scriptures marked ESV are taken from The Holy Bible, English Standard Version. ESV® Text Edition: 2016. Copyright © 2001 by Crossway Bibles, a publishing ministry of Good News Publishers. All rights reserved.

Scriptures marked NKJV are taken from the New King James Version® of The Holy Bible. Copyright © 1982 by Thomas Nelson. Used by permission. All rights reserved.

Scriptures marked EXB are taken from The Expanded Bible, Copyright © 2011 Thomas Nelson Inc. All rights reserved.

Scriptures marked ICB are taken from the International Children's Bible®. Copyright© 1986, 1988, 1999, 2015 by Tommy Nelson™, a division of Thomas Nelson. All rights reserved.

Scriptures marked MSG are taken from The Message Bible. Published by permission. Originally published by NavPress in English as THE MESSAGE: The Bible in Contemporary Language copyright 2002 by Eugene Peterson. All rights reserved. (The Message Bible Online)

Scriptures marked ERV are taken from the Easy-to-Read Version (ERV) of the Holy Bible. Copyright © 2006 by Bible League International. All rights reserved.

Published by:
Peter Bonadie Ministries Inc.
770 Park Place
Brooklyn, NY 11216
Tel: 347-281-9059
Email: apostlebonadie@gmail.com
www.peterbonadieministries.org

Editing & Layout by:
Joanne Nicolls
joannenicolls1@yahoo.com

Cover Design by:
Marlon Nicolls & Associates
www.marlonicolls.com
Tel: 347-459-4027

DEDICATION

This book is dedicated to 'Kingdom Millionaires'. In my definition, a 'Kingdom Millionaire' is one who may not as yet have a million dollars in equity or spendable cash, but they are the righteous who are entering the marketplace of life with a kingdom agenda and are determined to build wealth while playing by God's rules. They intend to make Jesus Lord in the final frontier, the world of money. They are money-magnets and millionaire-makers. May these words help you to cultivate new moral habits or, at least, build on those that Kingdom Millionaires are already cultivating. I declare that you are about to enter your million-dollar flow.

ACKNOWLEDGEMENTS

I want to acknowledge the friends that I have had over the years that have inspired me to go to my wealthy place. Mostly, I must mention Mr. Patrick and Michael Maser. These men are Senior Vice-Presidents of a major Network Marketing company that's helping thousands around the world to achieve their dreams.

My tenure with them taught me some powerful lessons, such as: when prosperity comes, I must keep the bar down. They cautioned me not to get into hype, and so, paralyze my efforts. They also advised that no man can amass a fortune while living on an emotional roller-coaster. They emphasized to me that I must help others to get rich and I would be paid for doing so. The most powerful statement that Patrick made to me was this incredible truism: *"People do not care how much you know until they know how much you care."* That statement is believed to have originated from President Theodore Roosevelt, but they made it known to me. Thanks, friends, for the amazing example you have been to me and my family. You have made me a money magnet and a millionaire maker.

CONTENTS

Dedication

Acknowledgements

FOREWORD

One of the major things about the last days that we live in is that it is the 'Information Age'. The age where people simply look to Google and other internet-based apps for answers to major questions in their lives. It is also the age in which the drive for success is seemingly unparalleled. Everyone wants to succeed and there is a general feeling that everyone can *indeed* succeed because of the abundance of information available to us through the internet and social media.

The "almighty" internet is, for many, the remedy for all things. This has led to even Christians increasingly moving away from seeking God for answers because their phones and computers seem to have it all. Hence, in general, we see the masses moving further and further away from God and His Word for solutions to the social ills of our societies and the major things that hinder us from succeeding in life.

This is why I want to thank Dr. Peter Bonadie for writing this book: "*10 Habits That Block Success*".

While most of us look outward to find the things hindering us from succeeding, Dr. Bonadie has greatly stimulated a high level of introspection and reflection through this book, to cause us not

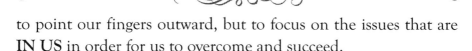

to point our fingers outward, but to focus on the issues that are **IN US** in order for us to overcome and succeed.

He starts out by hitting the nail on the head: that humanity's problem is primarily caused by OUR INIQUITY, period!

This means that man's answer lies in Jesus Christ and not Google and the internet. **He** is the one who was bruised for our iniquities (Isaiah 53:4-5), and the gospel message is simply showing us that 'in Him' and 'through Him' we have the victory (Romans 3:21-25; 5:8-17).

Dr. Bonadie, as a wise master-builder and a phenomenal teacher of the Word of God, meticulously takes us on a gripping journey through the Scriptures.

Our key problems are mainly internal, and not external. They are primarily the result of ungodly habits that we have developed over years as we have followed the dictates of our flesh and not embraced the delivering power of God, which is in His Word.

While we know that there's an adversary called the devil, we must realize that he is powerless against anyone who has embraced God's principles of success and continually applies them in order to overcome every ungodly habit of the flesh.

As I went through the chapters, I can summarize the book as a New Testament perspective to the Ten Commandments. You might say, "But we are not under the law but under grace!" Beloved, be aware that the law was ordained to guide us in life, and it is the grace of God that enables us to do those things that please the Lord, which the law recommends. Remember, that as 'New Creatures in Christ', God's laws or 'Will' has been written in our hearts so that we can please God. In the Old Testament times, no man had the capacity to please God fully because they were

spiritually dead. However, as a result of the redemptive work of Christ, we now, through God's grace, have what it takes to do the things that bring God pleasure and consequently succeed on earth.

Beloved, this book will revolutionize your life, because it directs us and points us to God's Word. It will literally "bind you to God" so you would not be bound to godless habits. Remember what David said in the 119th Psalm, and what Jesus said to the Jews that believed in Him:

> *"⁹Wherewithal shall a young man cleanse his way? by taking heed thereto according to thy word... ¹¹ Thy word have I hid in mine heart, that I might not sin against thee." – (Psalm 119:9, 11)*

> *"³¹ Then said Jesus to those Jews which believed on him, If ye continue in my word, then are ye my disciples indeed; ³² And ye shall know the truth, and the truth shall make you free." – (John 8:31-32)*

I believe that this book is a phenomenal tool in the quest to fulfill the above Scriptures and live successfully on earth.

Once again, I want to thank Dr. Bonadie for writing this classic and providing a "victory-guaranteed tool" for God's people.

—Dr. David Ibeleme
Victorious Faith Ministries
Trinidad & Tobago

INTRODUCTION

INIQUITY is the greatest hindrance to an individual, a family or a nation. It is in a category over and above a transgression, that is, the breaking of the law of God even when you are not aware of it.

'Iniquity' is pronounced 'in-ik'-wi-ti', and its most common Hebrew translation is *'avon'*. Etymologically, it is customary to explain it as meaning literally "crookedness," "perverseness," i.e. evil regarded as that which is not straight or upright; "moral distortion". Another word frequently translated 'iniquity' is *'awen'*, literally defined: "worthlessness," or "vanity," hence, "naughtiness," "mischief."

In the New Testament, the Greek word for 'iniquity' is *'anomia'*, "the condition of one without law," "lawlessness." The Encarta Dictionary (North America) defines 'iniquity' as 1. "Injustice" or "Immorality." 2. An "Immoral act." 3. "Gross immorality" or "Gross injustice," "Wickedness." 4. A sin.

Iniquities have the ability to stop the power of God in our lives. It is not that they are more powerful than the power of God; it is **how** God operates. When He sees these things operating in our lives, He does not move favorably on our behalf.

When God gave us His commandments and His laws, His intention was that they would be the instruments used by us in everyday decisions that ultimately shape our habits. It can be compared to the sailor out at sea being dependant on the compass to help guide the ship to a desired destination. Likewise, we need the laws of God to help us make wise decisions that lead to success in our lives.

There are principles and laws established in the Word of God to help us to understand iniquities and how they can destroy our lives. God gave His laws to Moses in Exodus chapter 20, so the people could be taught how to live.

The word "law" implies a "principle." In other words, God was saying: *"Teach the people* **principles***."* The word "principle" can easily be translated "science." Traditionally, we have been taught that science and the Bible are contradictory philosophies. However, true science will **always** prove the **accuracy** of the Bible. Where science is true, it will always establish God as being Sovereign. I have taken the liberty to add "science" to that equation, because it is the true understanding of nature, the way things are and how they function.

The laws of nature are reliable. If God says you will die if you do a particular thing, it is a reliable principle. It may be that you could avoid certain detrimental things from occurring in your life if you follow these laws.

The Bible says, *"Give and it shall be given unto you..."* (Luke 6:38). Likewise, *"...do to others what you would have them do to you..."* (Matthew 7:12). You see, there are laws that govern the reason why things happen to us. Therefore, if you understand science or the principle, you could determine the results.

God tells us to do what He says, and we shall live. The opposite of that is to disobey what He says, and we shall die; because we are breaking spiritual and natural laws. In other words, God gives us certain guidelines to live by and be successful. He wants our lives to be blessed.

In this book, I share 10 habits that block success as an exposition on the 'Ten Commandments'. Each description will hopefully help you recognize God's will for your life, so you will be able to receive all that He has for you. I also address the issue of accessing the blessings of God. Clearly, any study of the Word of God will show His readiness and willingness to bless His children.

The Bible reveals things that hinder the flow of God's blessings called 'habits'. There are certain habits that we practice from time to time that block our blessings, and no matter how much we pray or confess, they block the power of God and the blessings of God from coming upon us.

Obeying God's principles gives us access to His provisions and blessings. You must understand the principles in the Word of God that are designed for your success. When you obey God's principles, you access His provisions and blessings over your life.

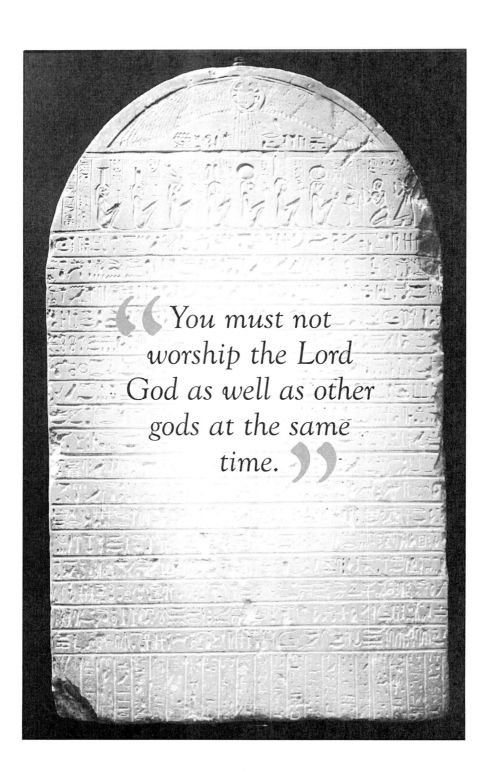

You must not worship the Lord God as well as other gods at the same time.

Denying God's Exclusive Right to Rule Your Life

Foundation Scripture
"You shall have no other gods before me."
(Exodus 20:3, NIV)

The practice of idolatry is a very serious iniquitous habit. In fact, it is so serious, that it is the first offense God put on the list: **'the worship and service to false gods'**. Not only that, but God says you must **not** have any other gods **before** Him; that is, anything held in higher esteem than Him. He also says you should not have any other gods **beside** Him. That means there are some Christians who may love God and desire to serve Him, but there are other gods they want to serve at the same time. This is absolutely not acceptable to the Most High God!

No Other gods

God says in Exodus 20:3, *"You should have* **no other gods** *before Me!"* The practice of worshiping false gods creates a

flow of demonic activity in the spirit realm and brings the curse of God over your lives...actually, it is retribution for idolatrous behavior. The Bible warns us that God takes the issue of idolatry very seriously... He says you must **not** have any other gods before Him; there must not be any other god in your life that is treated with greater commitment and allegiance than the God of Heaven.

You should not be worshiping God and praying to Mary at the same time. Now I have nothing against the Virgin Mary and I respect her, but the Bible forbids us from praying to any creature other than the God of Heaven. You are not supposed to have a statue of Mary, or any other idol for that matter. You are forbidden by the God of the Bible to place any other god **BEFORE** Him, nor are you allowed to have a god **BESIDE** Him. That means you must not worship God as well as other gods at the same time. You cannot be a Christian and a Buddhist at the same time. You cannot have a little idol in your bedroom hidden away, while attempting to serve the Living God.

I have read many stories of people who have idolatrous objects around their houses; some experience the negative impact of curses and spells until they throw these items out of their house. It has been observed that curses break immediately after the removal of the idol it is associated with. False gods can be in the form of a 'guru' somewhere in a closet, or a special artifact in a room of your home, hidden in your cupboard or placed on a shelf. If this is the case, you may end up having the 'true' God and a 'false' god together. God does not like being **alongside** any other gods, because He is a jealous God.

2

In 1 Samuel chapter 5, the story is told how the Ark of the Covenant representing the God of Heaven was stolen by the Philistines and placed inside the Temple of the Philistine god whose name was Dagon. The chapter portrays a picture of people having two gods:

- The God of the Bible; and

- The Dagon god.

The Philistines chose to put the God of Heaven next to Dagon, an act totally forbidden by God, and the consequences were quite profound. Here's what happened as recorded in 1 Samuel chapter 5:1-5.

> "*¹After the Philistines had captured the ark of God, they took it from Ebenezer to Ashdod. ²Then they carried the ark into Dagon's temple and set it beside Dagon. ³When the people of Ashdod rose early the next day, there was Dagon, fallen on his face on the ground before the ark of the LORD!*"

(Dagon, the god of the Philistines was slain; he laid dead before the God of Israel, the Lord of hosts! They took Dagon and put him back in his place).

> "*⁴But the following morning when they rose, there was Dagon, fallen on his face on the ground before the ark of the LORD! His head and hands had been broken off and were lying on the threshold; only his body remained.*"

(God amputated Dagon).

"⁵That is why to this day neither the priests of Dagon nor any others who enter Dagon's temple at Ashdod step on the threshold." (NIV)

Their actions can be compared with those of our age. Just as the Philistines made the mistake of placing the true and Living God **'beside'** their god, Dagon—much to their regret—in the same way it is quite possible for this generation to have other gods in their lives; gods that are dead and cannot be compared with the God of Heaven, the One who made heaven and earth. Also, in a similar manner, it is quite possible to reap a negative outcome for this misdemeanor, just as they did.

Only One Master

You cannot have any other gods beside the Most High God. If you put them together, you are looking for trouble! You do not know whom you are dealing with! When the Philistines went into the temple, Dagon's legs were in front of the threshold of the door. They could not figure out how a big, robust-looking god like Dagon, when put **beside** a little box representing the God of Heaven, could bring about such devastating results. Imagine this impressive, god-like image had enough sense to fall upon his face to the earth before the Ark of the Lord. They came back and met Dagon 'bowing down in worship' to the True and Living God. They put him back up and when they came the next day, his feet were by the door. Now how could that happen? It appears that Dagon was trying to RUN!!!

God sent a clear message to this god: *"I don't want you **beside** ME!"* The Bible says we are not to serve both God and Mammon. You cannot serve two masters at the same time. Either you will love one and hate the other, or you will hate one and love the other.

Now notice what happened in verse 5 as a result of God's public humiliation of their "god":

> *"⁵That is why to this day neither the priests of Dagon nor any others who enter Dagon's temple at Ashdod step on the threshold."*

They had to create another door to get in.

In continuing to recall this affair, we see that the Lord's hand was heavy upon the people of Ashdod and its vicinity because they had put another god **beside** the God of Israel. The people in Ashdod and the neighboring territories began to experience peril. The True and the Living God brought devastation on them and afflicted them with cancerous tumors because the Philistines had other gods **beside** the God of the Bible.

The people of Ashdod were in a frenzied hurry to get rid of this 'God' that annihilated the image they had worshipped for so many years, and who was now seemingly punishing them. They called together all the rulers of the Philistines and asked, *"What should we do with the Ark of the God of Israel?"* Their solution was to have the God of Israel moved to Gath—a land of **giants**! That is where Goliath was from. So, they moved the Ark of God to 'giant territory.' Perhaps

they found that Ashdod was a weak place and Dagon was an athlete, so they wanted a stronger environment to contend with the Sovereign Lord. The Bible says after they moved the Ark, the Lord's hand was now against the city of Gath, and He threw it into a panic. He afflicted the people of the city, both young and old, with outbreaks of tumors.

The 'giants' of Gath soon recognized that the 'God' this golden box typified, was not One to play with; and after linking its Presence with their city-wide outbreak of emerods, they did not want it anywhere near them! They hastily sent the Ark of God from Gath and chose the doomed Ekron to be its next stop. That village was also soon in an uproar over the devastation brought upon them. The Bible further states that as the Ark of God was entering Ekron, the people of Ekron cried out...

> *"10b...They have brought the Ark of the God of Israel around us to kill us and our people!"*

The people of Ekron pleaded with the rulers of the Philistines to:

> *"11b...Send the Ark of the God of Israel away! Let it go back to its own place or it will kill us and our people. For death has filled the city with panic."*
> (1 Samuel 1:10-12)

God's hand was heavy upon the people, and those who did not die were afflicted with cancer. The whole city had cancer and the outcries went up to Heaven. Imagine, all this 'avoidable' suffering and loss took place because the

Philistines were misguided enough to brazenly put their god **beside** the God of the Bible.

Food for thought!... Could it be possible that your home or church or city may be in bondage because of the worship of some other 'god' **beside** the true God of the Bible?

If you take a closer look, you may see some negative situations that have been repeating themselves in your life or in your family for generations before you. These curses may be attached to an idol on a shelf, above the refrigerator, or some other designated spot. Sometimes it may even be a family heirloom or a picture.

Some people think it is acceptable to have a statue of Buddha somewhere in their home, while making the excuse that, *"It's alright; it's just a piece of wood."* God said you are to have **no** regard for any other god: *"not* **above** *Me, nor* **beside** *Me."* The word 'god' is a generic term. It doesn't only refer to the God of the Bible. There is only **one True God**, but there are several 'gods'.

The Bible says in Joel 2:17: *"Why do the nations say, 'Where is their god?'"* Our God is in Heaven. He does whatever He pleases, but their idols are silver and gold, made by the hands of man. I cannot understand how man could be so deceived as to worship a god **they** crafted with their own hands.

'god' Makers

Some people carve out their god and then bow down to it. If you made the god, this means **you** are **'greater'** than the god

you fashioned with your own human hands. You might as well worship yourself.

The Bible says in Psalm 115 verses 5 to 8, that these images:

> *"...have mouths, but cannot speak, eyes, but cannot see. They have ears, but cannot hear, noses, but cannot smell. They have hands, but cannot feel, feet, but cannot walk, nor can they utter a sound with their throats. Those who make them will be like them, and so will all who trust in them."*

The God of the Bible is the only true and living God. Our God is not made from wood and stone. He is Spirit! There is no other God beside Him!

False gods

Some people believe in holding on to anything as their god. If you bow down to images made in the likeness of other human beings or of animals, even *'live'* animals and other creatures—either domesticated or those of the wild—this constitutes the worship of false gods.

In my travels, I have been to India, and in that country, there are some of the most beautiful people in the world. But, unfortunately, in India they worship a myriad of things, including cows! They have millions of gods there.

Idolatry and Idols

Some of the kindest people I have ever met are in Africa, but many of them worship demons and ancestral spirits, and

they make image representations of them. Also, when I was in Japan, they took me to an area next to a huge Buddhist temple (they claimed it is the largest in Tokyo), and at both sides of the entrance there are images of huge creatures, about 12 to 15 feet tall, that we in Christendom have traditionally come to suspect to be demons. But the fact remains: people carved them out. Whenever someone makes an image or any physical representation of a god, that image is called an 'idol.' God, the Sovereign Lord, is greatly opposed to idolatry.

Covert Disguise

I once saw a documentary about a lady being interviewed who was part of the engineering team that designed a lot of ghastly-looking cartoon characters and creatures that are used in video games and on television. These 'creators' are very conscious of what they are doing and are intentionally teaching children to have an appreciation for the supernatural, but an aspect of the supernatural that doesn't reflect the Holy God of the Bible but is of demonic origin. They covertly cause children (and adults alike) to play and interact with demons under the guise of a seemingly harmless 'fun' activity.

People sometimes carve out images that represent gods such as Buddha and Mary or figures of famous religious people and departed saints, such as Saint Augustine. The Bible warns us not to make any objects like that. To make idols is wrong, and to have them in your possession could mean that you have a demon in your house messing with your marriage; interfering with your ability to walk; getting you sick; causing miscarriages; blocking up blessings in your life; and wrecking the lives of your children, among other unfavorable things. Idolatry is a serious issue in the economy of God.

Idolatry hinders prosperity and creates poverty.

God is very displeased with idolatry. In fact, when you look across the nations of the earth, you will notice the effects of idolatry in certain countries. I am told of a South American, English-speaking country, Guyana. This country is rich in natural resources and very scenic with a vast rainforest, however, owing to the fact that its political leadership several years ago embraced witchcraft, this act placed Guyana under a curse and ever since she has been unable to fully maximize her economic potentials. Incidentally, Guyana's current political leadership, of Indian origin, worship the gods of their forefathers of India, thus once again showing that despite vast natural resources, idolatry will result in poverty.

Similarly, the Haitian economy suffers today because of the people's embrace of idolatry. Haiti is regarded as the poorest country in the western hemisphere, and I believe it is because many of their traditions are steeped in demon worship. It is widely believed that Haiti was dedicated to

Satan over 100 years ago by its leadership, but God would have "no other gods BEFORE Him!" Don't get me wrong. The people of Haiti are wonderful people. I am only trying to show how nations that forget God on a national basis tend to lose prosperity. The country is as old as the United States and they preached emancipation, liberty and freedom before the Americas, yet it appears as of the Americas are free, and Haiti remains in bondage.

The same is true for Africa; the richest continent in the world and yet the *poorest* continent. What is this strange paradox? The people are not 'benefiting' from its natural, God-given, resources.

The vast majority of people on the planet live in what is referred to as 'Third World' or 'Fourth World' countries across the '10/40 Window'. In these countries, poverty is at its highest. It has been discovered that many of the inhabitants of these regions worship false gods and demons.

False gods affect the economy of a people.

In contrast, the American civilization was founded on the Ten Commandments and a revelation of the God of the Bible. The very heart of this country is, "In God We Trust."

11

She became the most powerful nation, not just before our time, but also in the history of the whole world. There is no empire prior to the United States of America that was as wealthy or as blessed as the United States of America, notwithstanding our sins. I still join with those who say, "God bless America!"

Now, we have to face the fact that this has nothing to do with bias or with preference; it has nothing to do with being a patriot of your country. We have to face the issue that false gods affect the economy of a people.

The Western powers who once promoted God are now taking measures to annihilate Him from their public places. I urge these nations, including America, to recall how God provided for its people when they trusted Him. As we have seen the effects of Godlessness in the Third World nations, let us remain true to the holy God.

The Incomparable God

In the Bible, one of the names used for God is 'El Elyon'. El Elyon reveals 'the God who is incomparable'. It means He is exalted high above all gods. El Elyon is matchless and high and lifted up. El Elyon is absolutely in a class by Himself. There is no other God like El Elyon.

In Exodus 15:11-12 the Bible says...

> "11Who among the gods is like you, LORD? Who is like you—majestic in holiness, awesome in glory, working wonders? 12You stretch out your right hand and the earth swallows your enemies." (NIV)

Furthermore, Psalms 96:2-6 urges all of humanity to:

> *"²Sing to the LORD, praise his name; proclaim his salvation day after day. ³Declare his glory among the nations, his marvelous deeds among all peoples. ⁴For great is the LORD and most worthy of praise; he is to be feared above all gods. ⁵For all the gods of the nations are idols, but the LORD made the heavens. ⁶Splendor and majesty are before him; strength and glory are in his sanctuary."*

There is no God like our God! He is awesome, matchless, incomparable, and highly exalted above all gods. There is no God like Jehovah, and if God be God, then serve Him! The Bible says He is the only potentate, King of Kings and Lord of Lords! Glory to God!

God's commands require heart responses.

This commandment to **"have no other gods before Him"** is not a suggestion. These are not the 'Ten Suggestions'; they are the Ten 'Commandments'. God is not *suggesting* this; He is serious. He turned it into a command and when God turns a statement into a command, He requires a certain type of heart response from us. He wants us to take it seriously. He wants us to radically respond. There must be deep-seated

13

commitment to true worship and service to the Living God. A conscious decision must be made to dismantle every false god that you become aware of in your life.

A Prophetic Manifestation

As a little boy, I remember in my country of St. Vincent in the Caribbean Region, we used to have an image of the Virgin Mary located in a remote area. One day my father took me to see the big statue sitting on a rock. When I saw the image of the Virgin Mary, without hesitation, I threw a stone at it, and my father turned around and pronounced a curse on me. It took years for me to undo the effects of what my father said that day because I had stoned the image of the Virgin Mary.

Reflecting back on my life, based on my understanding now, the spirit that came on me when I threw the stone at the image was indeed the Spirit of God. I can reason that it was a prophetic manifestation of who I BECAME IN THE KINGDOM OF GOD. My radical commitment to truth and to God was foreshadowed at that moment by my instinctive hostility towards images that represent celestial beings.

I also recall another incident that happened on the island in which one man was praying in the name of Jesus and another guy came up and started to curse the man, asking, "Why are you trying to go straight to Jesus? You are supposed to pray to His mother and when you pray to His mother, she will beseech Him for you!"

The man who prayed in the name of Jesus tried to prove his point to the opposing gentleman, but soon ceased what appeared to be a futile effort. One day the disagreeable guy got so sick, that the 'Jesus-praying' guy who was accused of praying in error, came over and asked him, "What would you like me to do for you?" He said, "Could you take me to the doctor?" The praying man saw an opportunity to prove his point and smugly said, "No, I will take you to his mother. You don't need the doctor; you need the doctor's mother."

If you are in a home that is firmly committed to idols, it would be advisable that you leave. That's why God called Abraham out of his father's house. God had a plan for Abraham's life, but that plan could have been ruined if he remained in his father's house in which there were false gods. Abraham's father was a maker of idols, therefore, God commanded him to come out of his father's house (Genesis 12:1). It is not because God didn't love Abraham's father, but that house was practicing idolatry, which is an abomination to God.

History has shown that in the Middle-Eastern region of the world, the sons would usually continue the trade of their fathers. But when it came to Abraham, God had other plans. God spoke to him in Genesis 12:1:

> *"¹ Go from your country, your people and your father's household and go to the land I will show you."*

Now, I am not teaching rebellion. If you are a young person whose mother or father has some idols in a room somewhere in your home, you must pray for God to get you out...fast! You do not have the authority to get rid of their idols when

your parents are not at home. That may be a prophetic thing to do, but the problem is, they may not understand your actions, thus, resulting in you reaping some 'not-so-nice' consequences. Furthermore, they may just go and get new ones to replace the ones that you discarded or destroyed. But the Bible says that we are to get out from under that spirit.

How to Handle Idolatry

Israel was warned not to follow the practices of nations in the same manner that they worshipped false gods. How, then, are we to deal with idolatry? In some cases, people were instructed to burn their articles of worship. Jews and Gentiles in Ephesus were not only guilty of idolatry, but also of the practice of black magic. After the Gospel was preached to them and many believed in the Lord Jesus, they destroyed the idolatrous items by burning them in a fire. In the Book of Acts chapter 19, verses 18 & 19 tell us...

> *"[18] Many of the believers began to confess, telling about all the evil things they had done. [19] Some of them had used magic. These believers brought their magic books and burned them before everyone. These books were worth about 50,000 silver coins."* (ERV)

How, then, should you handle idolatry?

1. Remove Yourself

You need to remove yourself from a house where the idolatry is accepted and practiced. If, however, the person who is doing it is the authority figure in the house, you would need

God's guidance as to how to handle the situation. God told Abraham to leave his country.

You may have dabbled with false gods and idols yourself. You may even have objects in your life that need to be dealt with! One should make this an important and urgent matter.

2. Do not consider the monetary value when getting rid of idols

According to Acts 19:19, the value of the items used for the 'curious arts' that were destroyed was fifty thousand pieces of silver. That's more than a hundred thousand US dollars in books. These were the religious manuals of false gods; their *'bibles'* in a manner of speaking. It was their writings on how to access these gods supernaturally. The Bible says they **burnt** them! And we must also do the same.

If you have books dedicated to 'false gods': my advice to you is to burn them! Regardless of how much you paid for them—even if you bought a book for a hundred thousand dollars—burn it! Do not say it is too expensive to destroy and put it down in the basement instead. The Biblical pattern is to utterly destroy it! That way you alleviate any temptations to go back to it. You cannot read ashes. Your attitude must be, "I am **never** going back to this and I am never ever, **ever** going to allow myself even the opportunity to go back to that!" Burn it! I believe someone reading this is about to get their freedom by complying with this instruction: **Burn It!!!**

Nobody can take care of you like the God of the Bible. You do not need any other gods beside Him. If you have Him, you have everything! There is no god that has power like our God. Any false gods you have will fall upon its face before our God.

You may say, "Pastor, you don't know how much I paid for this!" I don't *care* how much you paid for it. Burn it! And do not give it to anyone else either. Burn those bridges! Some people may not agree with such a drastic move and tell you **not** to burn them, but I am saying to you, "Burn those bridges and have no regard for their economic value." The Lord our God is not prepared to accommodate another god 'beside' Himself in your life!

Do not consult with false gods

Another thing we must bear in mind as to how we are to respond to idolatry is: **Do not consult with false gods.** Now I know that demons are often regarded as 'gods' to some people, and though they might not accept it, by this spiritual practice, they are establishing that they have an allegiance to another 'god' other than the 'God' of the Bible. This is one of the things that can block blessings in a community and an individual's life.

I remember years ago someone gave me a book that actually went into details about how to cast spells by accessing supernatural powers. I also learned that the root philosophy of the study of understanding 'self' and certain temperaments came from the occult. In order to cast a spell, they would have

to understand the person by deciphering their personality traits in order to know what they needed to do to manipulate and control that person by witchcraft. I also found this philosophy was being taught in churches.

Destroy Wrong Books

I had the book that was given to me on my shelf for a long time, and during that time I had great difficulty in school and couldn't break free from being a mediocre student. One day I was praying and while on my knees, my eyes zoomed in on it; I saw the forgotten *'black book'* on the shelf. The Spirit of God said to me: "Get up and move it. Get rid of it!" I did, and I remember from that moment there was a marked improvement in my academic performance. I rose to the number one position in my class.

Changes in your life should line up with God's divine plan.

Prior to destroying the book, I was always failing my exams to such an extent, that I would get the lowest marks out of everyone else in my entire class. It seemed as though whatever was attached to the book had locked off my brain

and subdued its retentive power and the ability to recall and analyze. Idolatry was damaging my mental powers. After obeying God's instruction, I was able to jump to another academic level once that stronghold was destroyed.

You see... if God says to destroy something, there has to be a reason why He wants it done. God has a plan for your life—a good plan— and He is trying to tell you the changes you need to make to line up with His divine purposes.

Some of you may have books that tell you what wicked things you should do to hurt other people, and you have them on your shelf or in a chest under your bed or some other secret hiding place. If that is the case, you are guilty of accessing supernatural powers and touching false gods. No wonder poverty has set in and the curse remains on your home causing barrenness and unfruitfulness. Or maybe you cannot hold a good job and it seems like nothing is breaking for you; this is because you have not dealt with this iniquity.

If you have any diabolical objects in your home, God is saying to you today, *"Burn them and get rid of them out of your house!"* He also says, *"Do not consult with them nor imitate their abominable ways!"*

Deuteronomy chapter 18 verses 9-10 clearly tells us:

> *"⁹ When you enter the land the LORD your God is giving you,* **do not learn to imitate the detestable ways** *of the nations there. ¹⁰Let no one be found among you who sacrifices his son or daughter in the fire..."*

The sacrifice of sons and daughters was a literal blood sacrifice that was given to false gods. I read an article where someone studied the roots of abortion and found that abortion has its roots in blood sacrifices to demons. There are certain women who are set aside to become pregnant to raise sacrifices for the worship of false gods, usually either to bless the vegetation, to help the troops going out to war, for protection and other fortunate happenings. But to look to anyone or anything other than the God of Heaven for good fortune is detestable in God's sight!

No Blood Sacrifices, Divination, or Sorcery

God warned Israel that if they wanted their grass to grow and crops to bloom, they did not need blood sacrifices to idols, nor to practice divination or sorcery. The word 'sorcery' in Greek is 'pharmicos', from which we get the word 'pharmacy', and it has to do with mind- and behavior-altering drugs.

An example of this form of 'sorcery' or 'pharmicos' can be found in some village cultures. If someone wanted a particular man to marry their daughter, they would invite him home and mix him a potion to 'catch him' or 'tie him' as it is referred to in some parts of the West Indies. They would get a delicious plate of food, 'well set' and laid out for the 'ketch'. Once the potion works, the victim would wake up the next morning feeling as though he is in a midsummer night's dream and surprisingly be madly in love with a girl he once hated! No one belonging to the kingdom of God should ever condone nor participate in such practices. They are despicable and violate the laws of God!

Witchcraft, Omens, & Mediums

God's word specifically warns us that we are not to engage in witchcraft nor consult with people who interpret omens, or a medium.

> *"10 Let no one be found among you ... who practices divination or sorcery, interprets omens, engages in witchcraft, 11 or casts spells, or who is a medium or spiritist or who consults the dead."* (Deuteronomy 18:10-11 – NIV)

A 'medium' is someone who claims to be in contact with spirits of the dead and 'mediates' between the dead and the living. They could take on a demonic personality that could actually imitate a departed person. How this works is that you may go to them and say, for example: "I miss my old Granny. It's been so long now, and I would like to talk to Granny," and when you open your eyes, the medium might say, "I see a bright light..." and then you hear a familiar voice saying, "I am here my child. What would you like to know?" "Granny are you in heaven?" you may ask curiously. To your surprise, 'Granny' responds: "Yes, my child. I have my own mansion, with my own walk-in closet and I want you to be here with me too." At that moment, in actuality, the 'real' Granny could be burning in hell if she wasn't saved.

The demonic 'Granny'-imposter may go on to reveal familiar personal details such as, "The ring I gave you with the little ruby stone is for good luck," which convinces the client that it was indeed her grandmother who the medium had contacted—though it was not. But that practice involves

dealing with supernatural powers; demonic entities that know exactly what to tell you in order to trap you! And it is absolutely likely to have adverse consequences!

Illegitimate access to the supernatural world is strictly forbidden

There are people who access the supernatural realm and touch other gods other than the God of the Bible, and because there are paranormal manifestations, they get addicted to such activities. The Bible says we are not to consult with spiritists, mediums or the dead. This is also referred to as necromancy. 'Necromancy' is to communicate with the dead. No necromancer should be consulted by Christians who belong to the kingdom of God.

> "12 Anyone who does these things is detestable to the Lord; because of these same detestable practices the Lord your God will drive out those nations from before you." (Deuteronomy 18:12)

You must be blameless before the Lord your God.

Diabolical sources

Some people may communicate with idols to prosper their businesses. I remember dealing with a family who had a very prosperous business. However, one member of the family disclosed the diabolical source of their 'prosperity'. She said to me, "Pastor, my mother appears to be successful, but I will tell you the truth. She has a little 'god' in a room and

takes food and flowers in there to that god; she spreads out the offerings and bows down and asks the god to bless her business. In fact, at the end of the day when food is left over from the restaurant, she would take some to the 'god'."

I knew her mother. When fellowshipping in church, she would praise the Lord with shouts of "Hallelujah! Isn't the Lord good? Look what the Lord has done!" However, she secretly worshipped a 'god' **besides** the 'True and Living God'. It didn't take long before things went wrong, because God hates this evil deed! The Bible says in Deuteronomy 12:1-3 to **break down** the false altars:

> *"[1] These are the decrees and laws you must be careful to follow in the land that the LORD, the God of your fathers, has given you to possess—as long as you live in the land. [2] Destroy completely all the places on the high mountains, on the hills and under every spreading tree, where the nations you are dispossessing worship their gods. [3]* **Break down their altars**, *smash their sacred stones and burn their Asherah poles in the fire; cut down the idols of their gods and wipe out their names from those places."*

God's instruction plainly states: **"Break down false altars....!"** In other words, if you have a god and you put it in a location in your house with a nice table set, and a luxurious red cushion on which to kneel, you must **get rid of the idol** and reconfigure the whole room. Do not leave the room like that. Smash down all the pictures you have on the walls; take them down; remove your altars; wipe them out completely;

get rid of them!!! Leave no stone unturned! Determine in your heart to never, *ever* again return to serving false gods! Instead, wholeheartedly serve the Living God, and Him only shall you serve. If you say the Lord is God, serve Him!

Some people turn to false gods to help them with relationships, money, sex, romance, etc. But, my God (the only True and Living God) shall supply all your needs! If the Lord is truly your Shepherd, as David says in Psalm 23, then you shall not want. He makes you to lie down in green pastures, He leads you beside still waters, He anoints your head with oil; He gives you 'running over' blessings if you will love Him and worship Him; if you will serve Him alone; if you will establish Him as El Elyon, the One who is incomparable; the One who is above all.

There is no god like our God... The Lord, He is God and there is none beside Him! You must not bow down to idols nor look to them for help... do not go before them with any prayers or petitions. Go to the Lord, the God of Heaven, and trust Him with all your heart!

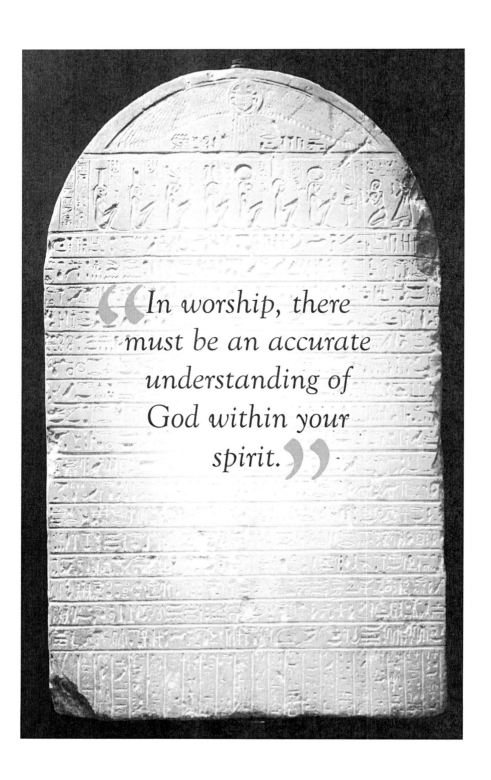

In worship, there must be an accurate understanding of God within your spirit.

SECOND RESTRICTIVE HABIT

Improperly Worshipping God

Foundation Scripture

"⁴ You shall not make for yourself any idol, or any likeness (form, manifestation) of what is in heaven above or on the earth beneath or in the water under the earth [as an object to worship]. ⁵ You shall not worship them nor serve them; for I, the Lord your God, am a jealous (impassioned) God [demanding what is rightfully and uniquely mine], visiting (avenging) the iniquity (sin, guilt) of the fathers on the children [that is, calling the children to account for the sins of their fathers], to the third and fourth generations of those who hate Me, ⁶ but showing graciousness and steadfast lovingkindness to thousands [of generations] of those who love Me and keep My commandments."
(Exodus 20:4-6, AMP)

Let us carefully examine the second iniquity called **'false worship'** since the first chapter distinguished the God of the Bible **above all** other gods; being the Only True God with none *before* or *beside* Him.

False worship deals with **constructing** an image to worship and bowing to it. We will look at Scriptures that differentiate

between bowing and actually worshipping. They go together, but there is a slight difference that needs to be emphasized.

Outward Signs of False Worship

False worship is a serious iniquity that may be **identified** by an attitude of coldness or apathy when people come to worship God. They show a sign of coldness by just standing there, expressionless, emotionless. Some people participate in worship and they never lift their hands, but if they do, it is usually at half-mast. There is no fire in their heart; no enthusiasm, no joy.

During the Old Testament days, it was forbidden to come before a king with sadness. That was a crime worthy of death. Everyone had to approach the king with joy and zeal in their hearts. Today there are some who attend Church with too much sophistication, affluence, and pride to raise their hands and worship God.

The apostle Paul says in 1 Timothy 2:8,

> "...I want men everywhere to pray, lifting up holy hands without anger or disputing."

False worship can occur when you are ashamed to worship God publicly, which indicates you may not worship Him 'privately'. When you have the proper construct of God in your spirit, it does not matter if your friends, relatives, or co-workers are present; you do not care who is in your midst; when you are mindful of what God has done in your life, you will praise Him anywhere and at any time. False worship is

worship that is cold and dry—a brand of worship God is not pleased with.

The Bible says in Revelations 3:16:

> "So, because you are lukewarm—neither hot nor cold—I am about to spit you out of my mouth."

The word 'spit' in the Greek means to 'vomit'. Cold believers can be described as people who are not on fire for God; they are lukewarm and tend to worship God on Sundays only. Lukewarm worship is an annoyance to God and it will drive His presence away from your life.

Lips without heart, is false worship!

The Bible says in Isaiah 29:13:

> "...These people come near to me with their mouth and honor me with their lips, but their hearts are far from me..."

In other words, you are saying something you do not really mean. You say, "Praise the Lord", but your heart is not praising Him. You may say, "Hallelujah", but it is not a sincere "Hallelujah!" Your words are not lining up with what is coming out of the dimension of your heart. You may

say "Praise the Lord" because it is the right thing to do, or because someone is looking at you or someone instructed you to. But it is not coming out of your own relationship with God: because you love God, you appreciate God, you are heavily connected to God, or because you have a deep yearning for His presence. It is lip, without heart!

What is Worship?

Worship is defined as *'being able to reach forth and kiss'*. It speaks of having intimacy with God. It means to *'recklessly abandon yourself in love and adoration to another'*. It is where you just 'lose it' because of how much you love this person.

I remember years ago there was a guy in our town who was madly in love with a certain girl, and because of his strong, uncontrollable passion for her, he gave her every dime he earned. I had never seen a man love a lady like that. Sadly, the feeling wasn't mutual; she didn't love him back, but she took his money. One day, I and a few other concerned acquaintances waited for him to come out of a store, so we could have a friendly chat to let him know what he was doing wrong. After we shared our observations and advice with him, he agreed to make the necessary adjustments to his actions, but shortly thereafter, he went right back to that place where the 'love of his life' was. He was willing to abandon his own reputation, his name, the respect he had for his life, just because **he was in love**.

That is what I call 'worship'. It is when your heart is so sold out to God, that you are ready to abandon everything else to

worship Him. You are willing to lose your own sophistication in order to fully express your adoration for Him without reservation. Sometimes we are more concerned about the opinions of people than with giving God what is rightfully His! This is what God wants; your whole being must be inside your worship.

False worship is irreverence; showing dishonor to God.

False worship is demonstrated during worship time when, for example, you are having a conversation with someone next to you or texting on your phone. It is an attitude of levity or lightness of heart. These things dishonor God and He treats them seriously because they are iniquities.

Irreverence is when you come before God with unconfessed sins, a lifestyle of uncleanness, and have not been immersed in the blood of Jesus. The Bible says,

> "³ Who may climb the mountain of the Lord?
> Who may stand in his holy place?
> ⁴ Only those whose hands and hearts are pure,
> who do not worship idols and never tell lies."
> (Psalm 24:3-4 - NLT)

You cannot be lying, stealing, cheating, and carrying out other 'crooked' deeds and expect that kind of behavior to be considered 'acceptable' worship. You must first purify your heart. Worship that is respectful, honorable and true to God is worship that comes from a pure heart and a clean spirit.

Worship without an offering is also false worship. Whenever you come before God to worship, you must have an offering. It would be prudent to note God's clear instructions in Exodus 34:20b which says:

"...No one is to appear before me empty-handed."

Though the directive here is quite indisputable, some people may hear these heavenly utterances and cast it aside, not realizing that disobedience to Scriptural instructions block their blessings. No one should draw near to God to worship Him without an offering.

Worship without a true revelation of God is false worship.

In worship, there must be an accurate understanding of God within your spirit. In John 4:22 Jesus had a conversation with a Samaritan woman at a well in Samaria. During the course of their verbal exchange, He brought up the subject of misdirected worship:

32

*"You Samaritans worship what you do not know; we worship what we **do know**, for salvation is from the Jews."*

No one can come before God without an accurate revelation of Him. We must become familiar with the God to whom the worship is directed.

To do so effectively, you must:

1. Have a private time of study and reading the Scriptures;
2. Fill your mind with a revelation of God;
3. Make notes; and
4. Pray daily, multiple times a day.

That's when true worship really takes place.

As we spend time in the Word of God, we become acquainted with the **'protocols'** of worship. In Psalm 100:1 (KJV), we are told to:

"¹ Make a joyful noise unto the Lord, all ye lands. ²Serve the Lord..."

How?

"...with gladness."

He is a good God! So, serve the Lord with **gladness**!

The Psalmist goes on to say in verse 4:

"⁴ Enter into his gates with thanksgiving, and into his courts with praise",

With what?

"...praise."

33

Then it says,

> *"⁵ For the Lord is good..."*

See? You cannot worship without revelation. There must be an **accurate** understanding of God if true worship is to take place. You cannot worship God effectually while having an inaccurate revelation of Him. Verse 3 says we must:

> **"Know** *that the Lord is God. It is he who made us..."*

In Mormonism, its worshipers do not realize their teachings have distorted the facts about the True and Living God. They teach that Adam is 'God' the Father. They are attempting to worship the 'Heavenly Father' while praying to 'Adam'. This is idolatry.

A bad attitude towards God has the ability to block His blessings.

There are religious groups that do not teach the truth about God. Neither do they teach that Jesus Christ is the Son of God. Instead, they have established vain philosophies. It is important to note that when you worship God, you are worshiping a **good God**! His mercy endures forever. You

cannot have this revelation and be quiet. You cannot know the mercies of God and worship Him 'half-heartedly.' A bad attitude towards God has the ability to block the blessings of God.

When you have false worship towards God, you are likely to be blocked from the best places to live and from abundance. Demons will find you friendly. Your place will be a habitation for devils. You will go around in circles without receiving God's bounty.

But when you have 'true' worship in your heart, when there's a desire for God, a fire in your heart for the things of God despite the opinions of others and regardless of what is going on in your life, then you will "know that you know" that God is a good God! You would have praises on your lips emanating from your grateful heart! When you worship God in this way, you will enter into a heavenly atmosphere. If this principle of God is violated, however, you will actually walk in iniquity and this sin will block the power and the anointing of God in your life.

God is Spirit; He's a living God.

Now in order for us to understand this iniquity and avoid it, we must remember that God is Spirit. Nobody is to have a physical representation of God or a mental construct of God

and bow down to it in worship. That's the first department of this iniquity; the construct of a false God.

Where there is a proliferation of false gods among the nations, it has been discovered that the people tend to walk in poverty. It is indisputable that such nations are—for the most part—afflicted with a numerous array of bondages and misfortunes. The images of false gods and the corresponding worship of same, encourage a rapid flow of demoniac activity. So, you must have the correct construct of God and I want to point out a couple of things to you about the Sovereign Lord:

1. God is a living personality, and so is deeply offended when we His creation do not worship Him in a correct manner.

2. He is manifested in the Father, the Son, and the Holy Spirit. However, worship is ascribed to the Father.

3. He has the ability to respond favorably or unfavorably when people worship.

The Law of Cause and Effect

There is a Law of physics called the 'law of cause and effect'. It is said that every time you step on the Earth it shakes, just a little. The 'cause' is my 'touch' or 'stepping'; the 'effect' is its 'shake'. In other words, something has to 'happen' in order to bring about a 'result'. However, the True and Living God **alone** is the exception to this rule. God is eternal, meaning, He has no beginning of days and He has no ending

of days. This is a strong theological, doctrinal position. Let me explain it this way:

Ormond James Bonadie is my father. I don't know who Ormond James Bonadie's father is, but my father had a father, who had a father, who had a father.... and we can go on all the way back to God. When you get to God, **nobody** made Him. The issue of God being eternal is not only defined theologically as the One who has no ending, but to be 'eternal' means He also had no beginning. When you got saved, your 'everlasting life' began. But God is eternal! There is no one like our God! Every other god had a beginning.

God is perfect. There's not a flaw in Him and He has never made a mistake. The God we serve is omnipotent, meaning 'all powerful', and He can do anything. God is omniscient. He has all science in Him. God knows everything, and He knows everyone, and He knows your name and address.

God is omnipresent; He is everywhere. Our living God, our perfect holy God is everywhere...everywhere at the same time, and to the same degree. My God lives inside my heart. He's big enough and small enough to live inside of me. Understanding the majesty of God is not just based on theological knowledge of Him, but on experiential knowledge as well.

Moses and Miriam had just experienced a grand display of God's power as He blasted a roadway for His people through the Red Sea in order for them to escape their Egyptian enemies. This miraculous incident spurred a song of worship from their grateful hearts in Exodus 15:11:

37

"Who among the gods
is like you, Lord?
Who is like you—
majestic in holiness,
awesome in glory,
working wonders?"

Their worship was birthed by an experience.

When we worship the Lord, not only should He be a 'theoretical' God to us, but we must also worship Him for what He means to us experientially. People sometimes say to Him: "I worship You for Who You are." Yes, but we must also worship Him **for what He's done** as well.

A Personable God

The God of Heaven is a very personable God. When I think about that and consider the salvation of my God, I **have** to worship Him. True worship pours out of a heart that is grateful; and I am so thankful for where God has brought me from, and for how He has taken care of me and my family. You see, you don't know, like I know, what God has done in my life. When I consider such a 'great' salvation, and how Jesus covered my sins and wrongdoings by His precious blood, praise flows easily out of my mouth! Despite who I am, who I was, or what I've done, He saved me!

The psalmist David had a very **personal** relationship with the Lord that comes across very clearly in his writings. He wrote,

*"The Lord is **my** Shepherd."* (Psalm 23:1)

... he did not say **"your"** Shepherd.

David's heart-to-heart relationship with the Lord showed up many times in Scripture. Another example of this is found in Psalm 40:1 & 2:

> *"I waited patiently for the Lord and He turned to* **me...***"* (again, not 'you'). *"...He turned to* **me** *and heard* **my** *cry!"* *"He lifted* **me** *out of the slimy pit..."* (NIV)

The Power of a Joyful Sound

God adds something to worship that I call the power of a **joyful sound**. After the spectacular parting of the Red Sea, Moses' sister, Miriam, took tambourines and some young ladies and, as freed people, began to dance and sing exuberant, joyous sounds of praise to the Most High God!

Prior to this, the people of Israel had spent hundreds of years in captivity. In the midst of their adversity they had lost their joyful sound. Their wicked oppressors mocked them and told them to sing the anthems of Zion, but the disheartened Israelites asked how they could sing the Lord's song in a strange land. However, the dramatic deliverance by the God of Heaven that day restored their joyful sounds of jubilant praise!

There is a correlation between the sun and joyful sounds. Let me just give you a couple of scientific facts about the sun. Scientists have discovered that light travels in something called an 'electromagnetic wave' that goes through the air. Scientists say that the human eye is unable to pick up the

entire color spectrum of light at the same time. But they also said that inside that electromagnetic wave of light is a 'radio wave'. They have found that whenever light begins to travel, there is **music** that goes with it; and what was the first thing that God created in the book of Genesis? "Light!" So, when I checked it out, the word for 'light' in the Hebrew is the word 'owr' [pronounced 'ore'].

The Bible says God is 'light'...therefore, it would be safe to assume that there was a joyful sound emanating from the very being of God. God said, "Light!" ...and there was. Science has also found that there is music coming from the starry bodies. The stars, the lights that pour down on the Earth, come down and hit us with music. When people invented 'pop' and other genre of music, it is not because they are so great, but because they just heard a little bit of the sound coming from the light of God.

A joyful sound offered to anyone or anything other than God is iniquity.

It is my belief that Calypso came from God. Pop came from God. Reggae came from God. Country music came from God. When God said, "Light be!" it was accompanied by a joyful sound pouring down on the human race as He released

all the diverse forms of music into the Earth. God wants to hear **His** joyful sound. And God is saying, "If you take that joyful sound and offer it to anybody or anything other than Me, it is an iniquity."

Other interesting facts about the 'joyful sound' can be discovered by examining the universal elements: wind, fire, water and earth. Wind, fire, and water produce a sound. And in the spirit, when any one of these elements begin to work, there is a sound. One of the first sounds that man heard was the breath of God – wind. When wind blows, it has the ability to animate dirt. The dirt begins to dance. It begins to twist and twirl. In other words, if you are hearing the joyful sound, it would be natural to respond by dancing. When God breathed into Adam, he got up and became "a living soul," capable of movement and dancing and joyful expressions of praise.

There is power to the joyful sound. God says that we are not to offer this joyful sound of worship to any image. It belongs only to God. Don't let Buddha hear the joyful sound because the power of this joyful sound will animate any object and even idols will respond. That's why people see images move. Some have seen images of Mary move and cry. I believe God is communicating to us, "Do not let any inanimate object hear this sound. Don't worship them!"

The Power of Sound

Sound carries qualities that are similar to light. Just as the human eye cannot see the entire spectrum of color that is in

light, similarly with sound, the human ear cannot hear every sound.

There are two dimensions to sound:

- Subsonic; and

- Ultrasonic

Some sounds are 'too low' for you to hear, and likewise, some are 'too high'. When it is too high, it's called **'ultrasonic sound'**. When it is too low for you to hear, it's a **'subsonic sound'**. Scientific studies have proven that if you hook up two thirty-inch speakers in a building and connect it to a first-rate power amplifier, you could actually physically shake the building. That is the power of sound.

The sound of worship in heaven is also extremely powerful. The Bible says in Revelations 14:1-3,

> "*1 Then I looked, and there before me was the Lamb, standing on Mount Zion, and with him 144,000 who had his name and his father's name written on their foreheads. 2And* **I heard a sound from heaven like the roar of rushing waters and like a loud peal of thunder. The sound** *I heard* **was like that of harpists playing their harps.** *3And* **they sang a new song** *before the throne...*"

This is not the old-time religion. It is a **current** operation of God. *"And they sang a 'new song' before the throne..."* So, based on what John saw in Heaven, when the people come together to worship in the presence of God, the magnitude of the sound is like that of a tidal wave. But what was it really? It

wasn't the water. It was the music, and it incorporated the sound of everyone worshiping in the presence of God. It was like a 'tidal wave' of praise coming to the worthy One who sits upon the throne, high and lifted up! The 'sound' of the multitude in worship was like a tsunami; like gigantic waves of water rushing into shore. That is how John heard it and described it.

You cannot come into the house of God and be quiet. You cannot just sit there pining away from hearing the sad song: the insult somebody told you, the bad news, the bills you have; that negative sound you're hearing will hinder your worship if you let it.

In 1 Samuel chapter 4, verses 5-8:

> "⁵ *When the ark of the Lord's covenant came into the camp, all Israel raised such a* **great shout** *that* **the ground shook**."

The praise of the people literally **shook** the land. Verse 6 goes on to say...

> "*Hearing the* **uproar**..."

That's what their enemies called the sound: an **'uproar'**.

The people of God gave thunderous praise to their Lord, but the Devil calls it an 'uproar'. This reaction can be compared to the 'Philistines' of today who say, "What's all this **shouting** in church about?!"

When the enemies of Israel learned that it was the presence of the Lord coming into the camp, the Philistines became afraid! The **shout** was a symbol of the greatness of God

amidst His people. Out of curiosity the enemy began to ask themselves concerning the earth-shattering commotion:

"What's all this shouting in the Hebrew camp?" In other words: *"I wonder what is going on over there?!"*

They learned that God's presence was in the camp. When we worship with a joyful sound, the enemy knows that God is in our midst.

Corporate Worship

When we truly worship God corporately, there is enough power to bring deliverance and healing to all the people. When we assemble to worship, we ought to leave with the power of God operating in our lives.

When all the Israelites worshipped God with a shout, the enemy cried out, "There is a God in their midst!" and reacted with extreme fear. The Bible says,

> *"...they became afraid..."* because they recognized that,
> **"God** *has come into the camp!!!"*

When we worship with a joyful shout, the devil is in trouble. Demons start screaming panicky words like, "Hey, we're in trouble. Do you hear that shout over there? We're in trouble! Nothing like this has happened before!"

In verse 8, the extent of their terror is evident:

> *"⁸ Woe unto us! who shall deliver us out of the hand of these mighty Gods?"* (KJV)

44

Do you realize what the enemy of God's people said?

"Woe unto us..."

This phrase means he accepts his defeat. In other words, *"See this thing here? I give up. I give up!"*

The sound of this kind of worship, I'm sure, causes the enemy to remember Calvary and the resurrection of Christ. The sound of this worship makes them remember the reformation; the day when a violent stroke of God came into the Earth. When worship comes out, the enemy begins to remember—in case he forgot—the mighty hand of our God.

Sound Demonstrated in the Fall of Jericho

The power of this sound was also demonstrated in the fall of Jericho in Joshua chapter 6. History has proven that Jericho was fortified by walls. The way this defensive barrier was constructed, it was not just **a** wall that surrounded Jericho, but **walls** (*plural*). There was an outer wall that was thirty feet high and six feet wide, made of raw stone and mortar. Then there was an inner wall that was fifteen feet away from that wall, which was twelve feet thick and thirty feet high. The outer wall was six feet thick, thirty feet high, and the inner wall of Jericho was twelve feet thick and thirty feet high. It was the most fortified city in Canaan.

Between the two walls there was a space of fifteen feet. The people of Jericho poured sand and stone to fill the gap to the top of the two walls. This strategy of combining the two walls caused the width of the entire wall to be over thirty feet thick

and very high. The philosophy of why they built it that way was in case an invading troop was able to crumble that outer wall, the rubble alone would form another wall, and it would still be difficult for the invading troop to come in freely. But even their masterful invention was not able to withstand the power of the 'shout!'

God told His people to lift up a shout on the seventh day. First of all, He told them to walk around the walls for six days without speaking. The idea of 'walking' here is not a 'casual stroll'. They had to 'march'! Now, could you imagine millions of feet hitting the ground, all day, for six days?! Do you know what God was doing? He was creating a **subsonic** sound. First, God sent a sound deep down into the foundation of enemy territory. When the foundations were weakened, they raised up an **ultrasonic** sound of a resounding shout! This sound, fueled by faith and obedience to the instructions of God, brought the walls completely down and produced a dramatic victory for the people of God.

A 'Ruah' Shout

In Hebrew, the basic word for 'shout' is the word 'shabach', but when I studied the passage of scripture about the taking of Jericho, I learned that in this case the sound they released was not a 'shabach'. The word God used for 'shout' in this instance is 'ruwa', [pronounced ru-ah]. And 'ruwa' means: 'to let go an **ear-splitting** sound'. The sound must be so sharp that you cannot even tolerate it yourself. It's a scream that is so high-pitched until you cannot hear its full sound in

the natural. It's an **ultrasonic** sound. This was the type of sound the children of Israel unleashed on the seventh day:

> "*²⁰ So the people* **shouted** *when the priests blew with the trumpets: and it came to pass, when the people heard the sound of the trumpet, and the people shouted with a great shout, that the wall fell down flat, so that the people went up into the city, every man straight before him, and they took the city.*" (Joshua 6:20 - KJV)

It was two types of shouts, really, that the people released that day: 'a shout' and a '**great** shout'. With the second shout the people were to declare a battle cry. A battle cry is saying what you want to happen to the enemy. It means to let go a shout, and then declare what you want to happen.

A Jericho Subsonic and Ultrasonic Effect

After that shout of declaration, the Bible says Israel walked in on level ground. How could you have a whole wall, forty-five by thirty feet, by thirty feet up, and yet walk straight over? Do you know what I think happened? The ground opened up, because of the [sub]sonic sound, and then the ultrasonic sound sent the 'impenetrable' walls down inside of the Earth. And God's people walked right in, every man, and they took the city.

If your perception of God is correct, something is going to happen to you in worship. If you understand that He is your 'man of war', you would not be inclined to just sit there without responding to His greatness and the fact that you are in the presence of the Living God.

A Lesson from David

Psalm 23 teaches us a lot from David and how he responded to what God meant to him at any given time. Use your imagination for a moment and picture David sitting out in the fields tending to his sheep. All the sheep are grazing, so he has a free moment; it's his lunch hour. He pulls out his harp in the cool of the day as he basks in the shade of a spreading tree and begins to soothingly play his harp and daydream. His imagery starts off with his familiar environment of sheep milling around on green pastures. Then he starts to visualize God as a caring Shepherd. A song emerges out of his heart, and he begins with the tender words:

"The Lord is my Shepherd..."

That is not theology. It is an experience.

"...I shall not want."

There is a rolling plain with green grass and cool, flowing streams where he takes his sheep to be refreshed. Then he says about his God, *"He leads me beside the still waters."* Look at the imagery inside David's mind. He's worshiping and he's responding to his perception of God as a compassionate, loving Shepherd.

Now, there may be times that sheep need to be moved because the pastures have dried up in one place and there is a need to take them to the other side to graze. A shepherd may have to cross a valley with the sheep, but in that valley, there may be some serpents hidden in the ground waiting to attack when

the sheep put their heads down to eat the grass. And so, to stop the snakes from biting their head, a shepherd would usually 'anoint' the sheep's head with oil. That would make the wool thick and it would repel the snakes.

David also perceived God as doing that for him. He says:

"He anoints my head with oil."

Another thing that David said in this Psalm was,

"He prepares a table before me."

I read that for years and did not fully understand it until I learned that in those days, if a fugitive was running from people who were trying to kill him, and he came up on a shepherd who had tents out in the field, all he had to do was run into the tent and he was guaranteed safety.

Based on history, the culture of the day was that the shepherd had to give him the best hot meal they had. It didn't matter who this man was, the cause of him running away, or whether he was a fugitive or not. Once he was able to get into the tent, the shepherd had to protect and treat him well. And when the enemy who was pursuing the runaway arrived, their customs dictated that the enemy could not come inside the tent. The enemy had to stand outside and watch the fugitive eat. He couldn't touch him **until he came out**.

David pictures himself like that fugitive and pens the words: *"He prepares a table before me, **in the presence of my enemies**."* But he puts a twist and a spin on it. He was not coming out of the tent, that place of safety. He says:

"Surely goodness and mercy shall follow me all the days of my life and I shall dwell in the house of the Lord forever!"

That way, God's protection is assured. Once God is perceived by you as your 'Good Shepherd', expressive praise comes easily! This is indeed a time to lift up holy hands and worship your Shepherd wherever you are. Lift up holy hands and exalt His Holy Name!

The iniquity of false worship must be put to rest!

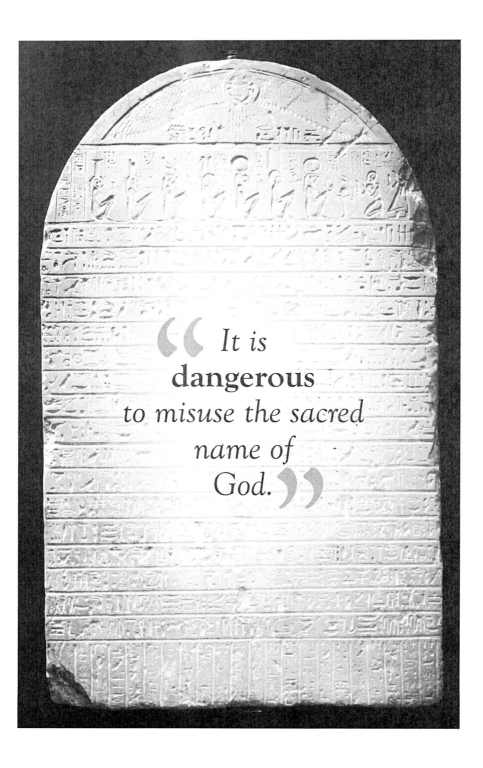

It is **dangerous** *to misuse the sacred name of God.*

THIRD RESTRICTIVE HABIT

Misuse of the Name of God

Foundation Scripture

"You shall not misuse the name of the Lord your God, for the Lord will not hold any one guiltless who misuses His name."
(Exodus 20:7, NIV)

The name of God is sacred, holy and to be revered. He forbids humans from using this name in swearing—whether in jest or intentionally. Evidently this is because the Name is to be used within the King's community to the glory of God and to establish His fame amongst the nations.

Before writing this, I prayed and told the Lord, "God, I'm going to get really graphic to bring the point across, so please forgive me while I'm penning it."

Some of us have a habit of just going around exclaiming, "Oh Jesus Christ!" or "Oh God!" There are people who use the name of 'Christ' to swear and it does not even occur to them that they are actually breaking a Divine Law. It is almost 'like' jumping' off a building. If you jump off a building, you can

kill yourself. So, when you break this law of the misuse of God's holy name, something goes into motion that works against you.

One never knows what blessings they have short-circuited by breaking this particular law. Let's say God had a supernatural blessing coming to you. God already promised He's going to bless you. But if you broke the law about the misuse of His name, He may actually cause your blessings to be received by someone else. You may never know what you missed. God wants you to avoid breaking spiritual laws so that you can be on the pathway to your abundance.

Let us look at another example of how this law works. Let's say you applied for citizenship in the United States of America, and your application is awaiting approval by the relevant authorities. You may have committed iniquity by misusing God's name the day before, but without you being aware, the immigration employee assigned to your case had worked all day, and the last thing she did before leaving to go home, was pull your file and put it in the 'Pending' tray to be dealt with first thing the next day. That night, for some strange reason, she got into a serious argument with her spouse. Let us say, as an example, that her husband was from Trinidad (no offense intended). Now, your file is the first case to be attended to when she reports to work the next day, but she arrives on the job upset with her 'Trinidadian' husband. Today, it just so happens that she opens the file on her desk and it's *your* 'Trinidadian' application. Because the nationality of the applicant is the same as that of her husband whom she was upset with, she doesn't even read it. "Bang! Bang!" She puts

a 'Rejected' stamp on the document and put it aside. It may look like an accident, but you forgot you misused the name of Jehovah two days prior, thus, triggering the unfavorable outcome of the application.

The Bible warns us:

X *"Do not be deceived: God cannot be mocked. A man reaps what he sows."* (Galatians 6:7)

That means you are affecting your tomorrow by what you do today.

Let us look again at misusing the name of God through the King James Version of Exodus 20:7:

"Thou shalt not take the name of the Lord thy God in vain..." (KJV)

Let's examine it from the Amplified Version:

"You shall not use or repeat the name of the Lord your God in vain [that is, lightly or frivolously, in false affirmations or profanely]; for the Lord will not hold him guiltless who takes His name in vain." (AMPC)

When God gave the Commandment "not to take His name in vain," He meant it! He said He would not hold the person 'guiltless' who does this. It is **dangerous** to misuse the sacred name of God.

There are several Hebrew words translated 'God' in the Old Testament: some by which God revealed Himself, such as 'Elohiym' and 'Yahweh'; and others which people ascribed as titles to Him to describe His actions, such as 'Jehovah Jireh'

when He provided, and 'Jehovah Rapha' when He brought about healing. I have personally experienced ascribing a name to God based on His actions. Years ago, God promised my father, Ormond James Bonadie, that he would have a son who would preach all over the world, and though my father died without seeing it happen, my mother could confirm, "God told your father somebody in his loins would preach to the nations." When this promise actually came to pass and today his son is preaching all over the world, I can lift my hands in praise and ascribe "faithfulness" to the God who kept His word. I call Him **"Faithful."** This is not necessarily His name, but that is who He is to me in this particular instance.

The word 'god' is a generic term. It is not a special divine word, but an all-encompassing term used in reference to deities. Apart from the True and Living 'God', there are gods of wood, gods of stone, gods of all kinds. Cattle represent 'god' for some people. In India, the cat is one of their gods; people worship rats and trees in some nations. All of these entities represent 'god' to their worshippers. But there is one **true** God...our God of Heaven is the **only** living God.

For all the creative work of His hand, He takes care of it.

Some of the key words translated 'God' in the Bible are:

1. Elohiym

In the King James version of the Bible, almost every time one sees the word 'God' with the "G" capitalized, usually the original Hebrew word is 'Elohiym'. 'Elohiym' means 'all-powerful'. It carries the idea of God being in covenant with His creation to sustain it. He is a covenant-making and a covenant-keeping God.

2. Adonai

In most instances, when one sees the word 'Lord' in the Bible with the "L" capitalized, then the Hebrew word is generally 'Adonai'. This designation for God is precious. It means that God is the Possessor of Heaven and Earth. Essentially, it refers to the sovereignty of God in the sense that He owns it all and gives it to whomsoever He chooses.

3. Yahweh / Jehovah

In Exodus chapter 3 there is an account of how God reveals Himself to Moses, a fugitive of Egypt. Moses was a Jew, born to Hebrew parents but was raised as an Egyptian Prince in Pharaoh's household. When God called out to Moses, he was in the 'backside' of the desert tending his father-in-law's sheep. God got Moses' attention, and when he turned around, he saw the startling sight of a tree that was on fire but not being burned! How could a tree be on fire without getting 'burned up?' Moses came close to see what was going

on. Then he heard the voice of God say, "Moses, do not come near, for the ground you stand on is holy ground."

Further dialogue ensues between God and Moses, and God told him that He was sending him to the Israelites who were in slavery in Egypt for centuries. But listen to what Moses said, *"When I go to the Israelites ... who shall I say sent me?"*

In other words, Moses was asking God, "Who are you?" And God answered him, saying, *"Tell them* **'I Am, that I Am...'"** (Exodus 3:14).

You see, God existed **before** the Heavens and the Earth. He existed **before** there was light and darkness, because He **made** light and darkness. There was nobody around. Angels only came on the scene when He created them. Before even 'time' began, God existed by Himself. In Isaiah 43:13 God puts it irrefutably: *"...**before** the day was,* **I am***...*"

The Egyptians had all kinds of gods and Moses wanted to know how to distinguish Him from all the other gods in the world. God said, *"Tell them,* **'I Am.'"** And that word in Hebrew is literally translated 'Yhwh'. It was pronounced as 'YAHWEH'. It carries the idea that "I will be what I will be." Though His essence does not change, His manifested form does. This piece of information is critical, because it prepares us to receive Him as a man when He manifested Himself in the form of the Lord Jesus Christ. Yahweh is the one true name for God. All the others are designations for Him that tell us of His greatness and worth. Let's look at some qualities of His sovereignty:

1. God needs **nothing** to exist. He doesn't need oxygen, He doesn't need carbon-dioxide, and He doesn't breathe air.

2. God does not grow old and He was never young.

3. He does not need food, a doctor nor a lawyer.

God was living happily by Himself until He made us. He was quite contented with Himself. There was nobody to say it was not good for God to be alone.

The name 'Jehovah' is explosive! It means that God is the only 'Creature' in the world who determines **His own** existence. Think about that. Your existence was determined by God. You did not make yourself a man or a woman; you had no choice in the matter. As a human being you cannot get up one morning and say, "From now on, I'm a lizard." You may dress like one, paint yourself like one, but you'll **never** be a lizard. You cannot determine your own existence.

Nothing or no one in the world, not even the Devil, can determine the form of their existence. God **alone** determines this. **He** decides what would be a dog, a cat, or a rat. **He** determines everything. You cannot change that! But an astounding fact to consider is that He determines **His own** existence. Before everything else was created, **He was!!!** He has no beginning and no ending...He is the self-existent One. So, He can take on whatever form He desires.

If God chooses to be a cloud, then He's a cloud. If He chooses to fly like a bird, He can descend on someone like a dove. God can be a rock. He determines who He wants to be. He is an awesome God. And it is common for Him to be given names that coincide with who He revealed Himself to be at any given moment. When God showed up as 'Jehovah' and He went to battle and fought for people and they won, they called him *'Jehovah Nissi'*, meaning: 'Jehovah is a warrior!' And then if they got sick and Jehovah healed them, He became to them *'Jehovah Rapha'*: Jehovah heals. If someone had a need and God showed up and provided, they may say, "Do you mean Jehovah meets people's needs? He is *'Jehovah Jireh.'*" God becomes anything that He chooses to be.

The God Who Is More Than Enough

God said to Moses in Exodus 6:2, *"I am the LORD,"* (capital "L" capital "O" capital "R" capital "D"). Now, in most cases, when you see the word 'LORD' in all caps, the Hebrew word interpreted is not 'Adonai', but 'Yahweh' (Jehovah). He said,

"I am Jehovah."

He also said,

"I appeared to Abraham, to Isaac and to Jacob as **God Almighty**," (Exodus 6:3).

The original word for 'God Almighty' is *'El Shaddai'*. 'El Shaddai' is 'the God of the abundant supply; the God that's more than enough'.

Your God is more than you will ever need. He is 'El Shaddai'. But notice He said, *"That is how I appeared to Abraham...but by my name 'the LORD' I did not make myself known to them."* (Exodus 6:3). Now, do you see the difference? He appeared to them, but never told them what His name was. God was implying that His name was a secret. Abraham didn't know it, Isaac didn't know it, "but now I am telling you Moses, what my name is."

Then He says,

> *"⁴ I also established my covenant with them to give them the land of Canaan, where they resided as foreigners. ⁵ Moreover, I have heard the groaning of the Israelites, whom the Egyptians are enslaving, and I have remembered my covenant. ⁶ Therefore, say to the Israelites:* **'I am the LORD...'**" (Exodus 6:4-6 NIV)

In other words, *"Tell them now, I am Yahweh."* Show them the sacred name, and by the revelation of the true name of God, *"I will bring you out from under the yoke..."*

> *"⁶ᵇ... I will free you from being slaves to them, and I will redeem you with an outstretched arm and with mighty acts of judgment. ⁷ I will take you as my own people, and I will be your God. Then you will know that I am the* LORD *your God, who brought you out from under the yoke of the Egyptians. ⁸ And I will bring you to the land I swore with uplifted hand to give to Abraham, to Isaac and to Jacob. I will give it to you as a possession. I am the LORD.'"* (Exodus 6:6b-8).

I will be
that I will be

Notice, God said, you are coming **out** from under the yoke of the Egyptians. What God was trying to tell the people is that once you get to know the power in the Name, there is no yoke, there is no bondage, that could hold you captive. If you understand the power in the name, there is no demon that can hold you.

There is power in God's name. It doesn't matter how big your problem is, it does not matter how long your journey has been, God will bring you out by His powerful Name!

Do Not Misuse His Name

As mentioned before, the name 'Jehovah' defines the very existence of God. It's the most comprehensive definition of the awesomeness of God. Once Israel saw the power in that name, the majesty in that name, their reverence for the name of God became unquestionable. It speaks of God in His ultimate sense of being, and it was not to be misused in any way.

He told Israel, *"Do not make anybody misuse that name, for I will not hold anybody guiltless who does."*

Now do you know what that is like? Could you imagine how I would feel if I go shopping and buy a tennis shoe for my son that costs $1,500, and when I look, the boy is outside running up and down in the rain, kicking 'tin cups,' with my $1,500 tennis shoes? Now that will get you mad, wouldn't it?

God says, because of the awesomeness in that Name, nobody is to take that Name in vain or desecrate its value. The word 'vain' means to be 'useless.' Nobody is to use that Name except there is a serious effect they are looking for. Do not use it frivolously, because there is power in that Name. Awesome power!

Nobody is supposed to use the name of the Lord in vain. The Bible calls it an iniquity. It is an iniquitous thing to use God's name in cursing other people. Regardless of how upset you may get with people or how grievous the offense against you, **never** use the name of God to curse other people, because God is not going to hold you guiltless. It's an iniquity that will block your blessing or your success. You should not use the name of God frivolously, such as in casual exclamations, "Oh God!" "Jesus!" If you are looking at a boxing match and a guy hits his opponent and you say, "Jesus Lord!"...that is considered using God's name in vain.

I remember years ago I used to hear a song: "For He's more than just a 'swear word'... more than just an 'I don't care' word." How can we use this Name so recklessly? This Name is too sacred and glorious to use in just simple exclamations. It is inexplicable—despite all the gods in the world—how so many people swear by the Lord Jesus. You often hear people exclaim "Oh Jesus Christ!" We should seek to avoid these loose exclamations because they are offensive to God and provokes a negative response that may inhibit or impede progress.

Jewish Orthodox Definition for 'Madness'

Some time ago, a curious gentleman asked a Jewish Orthodox Rabbi what it means, in the Jewish Orthodox culture, to **'sin'**.

The Rabbi's response to him was, "When a man knows the law of God with regard to the sanctity of God's name, if the person knowingly goes ahead and swears with the name of God, in the Jewish mind, that man is considered a **'crazy'** man." Their definition of 'madness' is 'somebody who breaks the law of 'Jehovah'. They treat it **that** seriously.

But we in the 'non-Jewish' world tend not to be as diligent when it comes to handling God's name with holy reverence. We can be lawless at times with respect to how we treat the name of God; taking His name in vain is primarily not viewed as a serious matter. No wonder, there is so much poverty around us. It is highly possible that the scourge of poverty is one of the negative results of this iniquity.

Do you want to know why almost everything the Jews touch turns to gold? In the Jewish mentality, they do not even use the name of God except when they are inside the Sanctuary. They treat God with the utmost respect. His name is reverenced; but, we behave as though God is our next-door neighbor, flippantly blurting out "Oh Lord!" "My God!" "Jesus!" with indifference and disdain. Now when the Devil shows up and you say, "In the name of Jesus..." the Devil does not even know whether you are serious or not, so he does not respond to you. Neither does **God** respond to you when you pray. It is not a simple issue; it is an **iniquity** to use the name of God in vain; to speak the name of God in humor!

You know, I like to hear nice humor, but some of the comedians have gotten to a point where they use a lot of

profanity and make a mockery of God. If you hear them using all kinds of foul expressions and humorous expressions about God and you laugh, do you know what you doing? You are actually agreeing with them. And the same judgment that is coming upon them is coming upon you for misusing the name of the Lord.

Now, when God said He would not hold you **'guiltless'**, He is actually saying: anytime you misuse the name of God you are perjuring yourself in the courts of Heaven. That is how it would be treated. It can be compared to standing in an earthly court of law and perjuring yourself or lying under oath. The judge would deal with you, and sometimes **severely**, for such an act. If you use the name of God loosely, when you go to pray, and you say, *"Father, in the name of Jesus I come to you..."* God is likely to shut you out. You are guilty of perjury and your prayers go unanswered. It blocks up your blessing. Perhaps that is a place where **all of us** need to repent and make a firm decision that we will be more vigilant when it comes to reverencing the name of the Lord.

The Power in the Representative Name of Christ Jesus

Under the New Covenant, the name of 'Jesus' is given. Now, how should we use this name? The name of 'Jesus' is a parallel to 'Yahweh'. His name is 'Yeshua'. Christ is the manifestation of Yahweh. So, under the New Covenant, we use the representative name of the Lord Jesus to exercise **spiritual authority**. It's a key to answered prayer.

In John 14:12-14, Jesus said:

> *"¹² I tell you the truth, anyone who believes in me will do the same works I have done, and even greater works, because I am going to be with the Father.* ¹³*You can ask for anything* **in my name,** *and I will do it, so that the Son can bring glory to the Father.* ¹⁴*Yes,* **ask me for anything in my name,** *and I* **will do it!**" (NLT)

You and I have to believe in the name of Jesus Christ so that when we pray in faith using His name, God responds to our prayer once our attitude is respectful and full of reverence.

In John 15:16 Jesus asserts,

> *"16 You did not choose me, but I chose you and appointed you so that you might go and bear fruit— fruit that will last—and so that* **whatever you ask in my name** *the Father will give you."*

There is power in prayer when we summon or invoke the name of Jesus. There is spiritual power that backs up that name. God responds to that name when we use it well. If you know the power in the name, then know that you are coming out of every difficult situation that you face. You are coming out from sickness in the name of Jesus! You are coming out from bondage in the name of Jesus! In the powerful name of Jesus, you are coming out from sin and poverty! There is no devil or any Pharaoh that can stop you. Your past cannot hold you! There is power in the name **of Jesus!**

We believe that we achieve through being authority

His Name Subdues the Enemy

The name of the Lord Jesus subdues the enemy. Subdues him! For, at the sound of that name, every knee shall bow, of beings on Earth, of beings under the Earth and beings above. If the devil is making a ruckus in your home, and if you don't know what else to say, use the Name! There is power in the name of Jesus! Demons tremble, in fact, demons **bow** at the sound of that **Name!**

I remember having some traumatic experiences as a little boy, when a demon would show up in the middle of the night and hold my throat, trying to strangle the breath out of me. I was fighting an 'invisible' entity, trying to get up, but couldn't. I remember hearing in Sunday School that there is power in the name of Jesus. And even when I wasn't walking with the Lord as I should, and I found myself under the pressure of the demonic attacks, I would say the name "JESUS!" in my mind, and somehow the demon would let me go. I was just a little boy at that time, but I was calling on the great name of the LORD. There is power in the NAME!

The Bible tells us:

> *"[17]And these signs will accompany those who believe:* **In my name,** *they will* **drive out demons...**"
> (Mark 16:17a - NIV)

The name of the LORD is a weapon of war! This is not just binding the devil; this is telling him where to go! If you use the Name, you can tell the devil exactly where to go. Out!

Out of your life, out of your house, out of your money, out of your church! **"Get out in the name of Jesus!!!"**

The name of the LORD is a supernatural cure for disease. An example of this is found in Acts chapter 3. One day, the apostles were going up to the Temple to pray, and they met a man who had been sick for many years. When the man saw the apostles, he stretched out his hand begging for alms. He wanted money from them, but instead, something unexpected happened. Peter said to the lame man:

> *"[6] ...Silver or gold I do not have, but what I do have I give you. **In the name of Jesus Christ** of Nazareth, walk."* (Acts 3:6)

And **he did!** He was healed!

This Name will make a cripple man walk! In the name of Jesus, cancer has to go. In the name of Jesus, AIDS has to go. In the name of Jesus, back disease, kidney disease, liver disease, eye disease, blood disease, heart disease, and every other kind of disease have to go! There is healing power in the name of Jesus!

Whose Authority?

However, an important point to note is that you must be authorized to use the Name. You **must** have a relationship with the Lord Jesus Christ in order to effectively use His name with authority and power.

In the Book of Acts, chapter 19, there were some young boys referred to as the 'Seven Sons of Sceva'. These young men

68

had seen the Apostle Paul preaching and casting out devils. They felt they could do the same thing, so they decided to practice by going to the home of a demon-possessed man. They were not Christians; they did not know Jesus as their Savior; their sins were not forgiven; they were not washed in the blood; but they went to **'try'** to use the 'Name.' Perhaps they wanted the fame; or to be able to brag about being able to cast out devils. Whatever the reason, in their attempt to cast the demon out, they said, **"In the name of Jesus whom Paul preaches..."** but the words were hardly out of their mouth before utter chaos broke out!!!

They had said, *"In the name of Jesus..."*, but He was not **'their'** Jesus, but **'Paul's'** Jesus. They did not love the Savior, nor were they serving Him, as Paul was ... but they said, *"In the name of Jesus that Paul was talking about...***Come out!"** The demon responded to them with a probing statement, *"Jesus I know, and Paul I know, but* **WHO ARE YOU?"** (Acts 19:15). The demons recognized that these boys were not **'authorized'** to use this Name against them... only the blood-washed saints of God have the legal right to use the name of the Lord Jesus.

I was reading the Biblical account of this story on an airplane one day and I laughed so loudly that it startled a Hispanic lady who was seated nearby. The portion of the text that I found funny was the part that said, **"They ran out of the house, naked and bleeding."** (Acts 19:16). The demon had undressed seven men. The demon was so bad, that in a couple of seconds, everybody was naked. That demon tore off all their clothes and beat the 'living daylights' out of those seven boys until they were bleeding; and chased them out of

the house in such a hurry, that they forgot decency. They did not care. They would rather be outside and in a shameful state than be inside with that *'thing'* that was in the building. They left clothes, shoes, everybody and everything! And they ran for their lives!!!

You do not have the right to use that name except Jesus is your LORD and your Savior; except you love Him with your whole heart. That's where the 'authorization' to use the Name of Jesus begins.

The Bible says in John 1:11 & 12:

> *"¹¹ He came to that which was his own, but his own did not receive him. ¹² Yet to all who did receive him, to those who* **believed in his name**, *he gave* **the right** *to become children of God..."*

It's only they that love Him and serve Him who has the **'right'** to use His name. So, when you and I speak, it is **not** in the name of Jesus 'whom Paul preaches', but in the name of Jesus, **my** LORD! **my** Savior! Do not take that Name in vain!

The Name of God is an Impregnable Fortress!

The name of the LORD is a fortified place of protection for His people! When you look at the Bible, it says in Proverbs 18:10:

> *"The name of the LORD is a strong tower..."*

It is a place that the righteous can run into and be safe. In other words, <u>the name of the LORD is a **defense.**</u> The name of my God is an impregnable fortress. A popular Hymn of yesteryear describes this sentiment beautifully:

> *"A mighty fortress is our God;*
> *a bulwark never failing..."*

A variety of troubles may have befallen you, but if you know the name of the LORD and you plead that holy name, I am telling you, there is no weapon formed against you that shall prosper, for *"Our **help** is in **the name of the Lord,** the Maker of heaven and earth."* (Psalm 124:8 - NIV)

God's Name is Worthy to be Praised

Now the name of the Lord should not be treated with contempt. It is worthy to be praised. Psalm 113, and verses 1-3 say:

> *"[1] Praise the Lord. Praise the Lord, you his servants,*
> **praise the name of the LORD.** *[2] Let the name*
> *of the LORD be praised, both now and forevermore.*
> *[3] From the rising of the sun to the place where it sets,*
> **the name of the Lord is to be praised."** (NIV)

There are all kinds of gods in this world, but there is **no god** like **our God** to whom **all** the praises belong. There are gods that people have to pick up and carry and feed. People worship various kinds of gods all over the world, but the Bible admonishes us that, "...from the moment the sun rises until it sets, everything it passes over **must** praise the name

of the Lord...for His greatness, for His mighty acts, for His wonderful kindness, for His mercy."

The great name of the Lord is not to be used loosely nor taken in vain. Instead,

> "*Let* **the name of the Lord** *be praised, both now and forevermore.*" (Psalm 113:2 – NIV)

(Hebrew)
Chattah - Sin
Awon - iniquity
Pasha - transgression

" Laziness
is an issue of
iniquity,
and it has the
potential to destroy
your life. "

Being wicked or immoral in
nature or character, wrong doing
evil, indicates a conscious
decision

4

THE FOURTH HABIT THAT HINDERS SUCCESS

Laziness

Foundation Scripture

"⁸Remember the Sabbath day by keeping it holy. ⁹Six days you shall labor and do all your work, ¹⁰but the seventh day is a Sabbath to the LORD your God. On it you shall not do any work, neither you, nor your son or daughter, nor your male or female servant, nor your animals, nor any foreigner residing in your towns. ¹¹For in six days the LORD made the heavens and the earth, the sea, and all that is in them, but He rested on the seventh day. Therefore the LORD blessed the Sabbath day and made it holy."
(Exodus 20:8-11, NIV)

In examining the ten (10) categories of God's Commandments of wrong-doings that will block the blessing of God over our lives, we now come to number 4: 'Laziness'. I want to lay the foundation for this bad habit by examining Exodus chapter 20:8-11 above. I want to show you how inside this commandment is the concept of 'effective labor'.

The Bible says, *"six days you shall labor."* The 'one day' in the seven has attracted more attention than the rest of the week.

He said, six days you shall labor, and rest one, and we are fighting over the *one*. We forget what He said about the other six days. We need to divide the week into two categories: 'a rest day' and 'work days'. You cannot say God's requirement for the seventh day is greater than His requirement over the six days. God did not say, *"Six days you shall work, and the main purpose in your life is that you rest on the seventh day."* The qualification to rest one day, means you must have worked for six. Most people want to rest six and work one. But He said, the only reason you have to take a vacation one day a week is that you must have worked for six days. Therefore, work has to be a divine issue to God. He is teaching us by this commandment that 'laziness' is an iniquity.

Work is a Divine issue to God.

Some believers have become very licentious, loose, and lawless, because they have not yet understood the value of 'law'. They keep the law when they're on the streets, they drive on the right side of the road, stop at the lights, they do all of that, but when they enter the house of God, somehow lawlessness seems to prevail. They believe that when they are anointed, there must be no order. It's amazing! The irony is that some believe that lawlessness is the work of the "Holy Spirit." The more anointed they are, the more lawless they're supposed to be.

Second Corinthians chapter 3 is a concept of great importance. That's when you look at the law and realize there are things hidden in every law that God gives that you must recognize.

The 'spirit' of the Law is the 'purpose' of the Law.

When you look at the Ten Commandments, you will see there are principles in each law that, if you're just going to keep the law as it is written, you will have difficulty in applying it to every situation.

For example, when the Bible says, *"You shall not murder"* or *"You shall not kill,"* (Exodus 20:13), if I wanted to be facetious about staying within the confines of that law as it is written, I do not have to kill you; I just have to beat you half to death and leave you *almost* dead, and that way I didn't break the commandment. That's what the Pharisees did. We must not miss what God is saying when He gave a specific command or law. Inside each law is an **'intention'**. The purpose of the commandment that says, *"You shall not steal"* (Exodus 20:15), is intended to protect people's property. So, anything that I may do that takes property without permission, or damages another person's belongings, breaks that commandment.

Keeping the 'Spirit' of the Law

You must keep the 'spirit' of the law—the 'heart' of the matter. For example, I remember when I was a little boy, my father used to beat me quite frequently and harshly. There were times when I threatened to run away from the house. One time he responded by saying "Well, get out of my house!" Now I may pack my clothes and leave my father's house because he told me to get out. But that is not what he was trying to tell me. I knew my father did not *really* want me out of the house. But because of my lawlessness, I packed my clothes and left. I followed his word as he said it and not the *spirit* of the *entire* conversation. I needed only to repent and demonstrate my sincere willingness to obey and honor him.

In the Book of Romans chapter 7, the Word says the law is holy, and the Commandment is holy, righteous and good (v.12). In addition, Romans 7:14 says, *"The law is* **spiritual***..."* It must be emphasized that the law is still relevant today as it was to those in the past, according to the Lord Jesus Christ.

So according to God, you are to work six days before you qualify to rest one. Because the one day you should give over for worship does not negate the tremendous and awesome value in working for six days. Work in the world as well as in the economy of God's kingdom is a strong basis for material prosperity and success in every form.

It does not matter what one's field of endeavor is. Even the super-wealthy have to put time in to maintain and guide the huge scope of wealth that they possess. There are people who make a great living by trading on the US stock market

which turns over an estimated one trillion dollars each year, or on the Forex Trading platforms which trade over three trillion dollars daily. They make millions, but often sit at the computer for hours to effect trades. It all has to do with a work ethic.

Good work ethics promote wealth and abundance.

If you do not have a good work ethic, you will never be able to amass large sums of wealth and walk in abundance. I don't care how much you pray and fast. I don't care how much you talk in tongues. It does not matter what miracles you may be believing to receive. The vast majority of the world must understand this. You will **never** be able to build abundance in your life until you develop a healthy work attitude. And let me emphasize this again, this is spiritual.

Some people believe that being spiritual is only about having the ability to pray and speak in tongues and preach. But a spiritual person is someone who applies principles of the Word of God to their day-to-day living. God is deeply committed to the construct of your daily life, as can be seen in Romans 12:1-2:

"¹⁻² So here's what I want you to do, God helping you: Take your everyday, ordinary life—your sleeping, eating, going-to-work, and walking-around life—and place it before God as an offering. Embracing what God does for you is the best thing you can do for him. Don't become so well-adjusted to your culture that you fit into it without even thinking. Instead, fix your attention on God. You'll be changed from the inside out. Readily recognize what he wants from you, and quickly respond to it. Unlike the culture around you, always dragging you down to its level of immaturity, God brings the best out of you, develops well-formed maturity in you." (MSG)

God wants us to spend most of our waking moments working to perfect the gifts and abilities that He has anointed us with. Our work ethic should be building our personal economy, as well as serving God's purposes in the community around us.

This fourth commandment deals with the issue of diligence and laziness. When we talk about laziness, we are taking into consideration some other definitions such as: slothfulness, inactivity, and idleness. All of these words can describe a person's attitude to work.

Some people think that "Work is evil!"

The Bible declares that laziness is an iniquity, associating itself with several other character flaws. God worked, so work is permissible.

"...Jesus said to them, 'My Father is always at his work to this very day, and I too am working.'" (John 5:17).

Many of the peoples of the world think that work is oppression, slavery, evil and bad; especially the people whose fore-parents were slaves and were oppressed on plantations. They tend to see work as being bad for them. For this reason, they also view the workplace as the environment in which oppression was brought to bear upon them. As a result, they either want quick returns on their efforts, or lean towards 'get-rich-quick' schemes. They may even become critical of the wealthy and the hard-working ones. This ought not to be! Work is **not** evil or bad; in fact, it is a **good** thing. By the rewards of our work we are able to feed our families, build businesses, contribute to our nation's GDP, express our God-given talents and abilities, among other gratifying things.

Work is a maintenance utility mandated by God.

In Genesis 2, verse 2, *"God had finished the work..."* God then took a righteous man, Adam, and told him to work **before** he sinned against God. Work is not as a result of sin. People

think hard work is a result of sin, but God gave work to a righteous man. Therefore, righteous people should work; it is a "maintenance utility." The Bible says in Genesis chapter 2 verse 15,

> *"The LORD God took the man and put him in the Garden of Eden to work at it and to take care of it."*

God intended that Adam should maintain the value and the appearance of the Garden of Eden. He had to have a solid attitude to work in general, otherwise, trees would overrun the Garden, or it would not be a place where he could sleep comfortably. <u>If God blesses you with anything, you are going to have to maintain it</u>. Work is designed for maintenance. Whatever assets you have, if you do not work, you will lose them. So, God gave man **work** to maintain the Garden; and He also expects us to work today.

Going the Extra Mile; Doing More Than Expected

<u>Work was intended to be creative</u>. God says be 'fruitful' or, in other words, be 'creative'. You can tell when a person is lazy. Just ask them on Monday to move a plant and put it in a certain place, and on Tuesday put it back. They may do what you ask, but nothing more! Now you have to be a really slothful and lazy person to pick the plant up, notice it needs watering, but because you were not specifically **told** to water the plant, all you do is relocate it as instructed. After a while, because the lazy person was not willing to do more than was directed, you'll most likely be picking up the pot *without* a

plant in it as it died from lack of care. That only happened because the person was told to "pick it up from there and put it back there" and an attitude of slothfulness determined doing just that, and not going the extra mile to water it.

There are some people like that. They would clean the kitchen and see that the living room is dirty, but because they were told to clean the kitchen, they would not touch the living room to tidy it up.

This concept of the extra mile is powerful. When practiced, it raises your "stock" at the market place, and you increase in value to your employers. We do this, not just to make money, but for the effective development of 'Character'. What is the place where we are challenged to be considerate, honest and cooperative? These are powerful character traits. The attitude of "not a penny less or a penny more" is one that makes a person ugly to coworkers and employers.

Work is needed for human sustenance.

If God is to get the abundance of wealth and blessing into your life, you must learn these principles. The Bible indicates that work is needed for human sustenance. It clearly states in 2 Thessalonians 3:10,

"...If anyone is not willing to work, then he is not to eat, either." (AMP)

Parents sometimes encounter this problem with lazy children in their home. There is something called 'tough love'. You must make them earn things, even if you have to save the money up for them later on. But teach them the importance of duty and work and routines.

The Bible says in Proverbs 12:27 that *"a lazy man does not roast his game."* He's too tired to cook! I once heard a man say that he was too tired to *laugh*. Some people take it to ridiculous levels. But seriously, though, the Bible says if a man does not work, he should not eat. If we follow these guidelines, we are likely to develop a lawful expectation for a corresponding return on our efforts and investments. Paul teaches this principle to working spiritual leaders. Regarding the issue of serving pastors and apostles, he speaks of having an expected return as a lawful desire. Let us examine the following verses of scripture:

> *"³ This is my [real ground of] defense (my vindication of myself) to those who would put me on trial and cross-examine me. ⁴ Have we not the right to our food and drink [at the expense of the churches]? ⁵Have we not the right also to take along with us a Christian sister as wife, as do the other apostles and the Lord's brothers and Cephas (Peter)? ⁶Or is it only Barnabas and I who have no right to refrain from doing manual labor for a livelihood [in order to go about the work of the ministry]? ⁷ [Consider this:] What soldier at*

any time serves at his own expense? Who plants a
vineyard and does not eat any of the fruit of it? Who
tends a flock and does not partake of the milk of the
flock? *⁸ Do I say this only on human authority and as*
a man reasons? Does not the Law endorse the same
principle?" (1 Corinthians 9:3-8 AMPC)

Another important fact we should know about 'laziness' is
that it is associated with 'wickedness'. Jesus told a parable
in Matthew chapter 25 about a servant who was not diligent
when it came to his work regarding his master's investments.
That servant was called, 'wicked' and 'lazy' as recorded in
verse 26:

> *"You wicked, lazy servant! So you knew that I harvest*
> *where I have not sown and gather where I have not*
> *scattered seed?"*

A lazy person is a wicked person in the economy of God. I
am not talking about the person who is trying to find work; it
is about the person who does not **want** to work and does not
know how to keep a job by their own diligence. So, in the
sight of God, a lazy person is considered 'wicked'; meaning,
it hurts others. 'Wickedness' denotes hurting other people.
When you are lazy, your actions cause others pain.

A lazy person is a wicked person in the economy of God.

Laziness and Gluttony

The Word of God also associates 'laziness' with 'gluttony', as seen in Titus 1:12:

> *"One of Crete's own prophets has said it, 'Cretans are always liars, evil brutes,* **lazy gluttons.***'"*

Laziness does bring on gluttony. Gluttony is 'greed' or 'excessive eating'. A lazy person does not want to work to eat, but, greedily depends on others to provide food for them. In Proverbs chapter 6, verses 6 to 8, the author points the sluggard to the 'ant' as an example to eradicate their 'sluggish' ways and teach them diligence.

> *"⁶Go to the ant, you sluggard; consider its ways, and be wise! ⁷It has no commander, no overseer or ruler. ⁸Yet is stores its provisions in summer and gathers its food at harvest."*

The Bible is speaking directly here to the lazy man, "Go to the ant you sluggard..." and do what? *"...consider its ways and be wise."* Get the point: a lazy man 'lacks initiative'. A lazy person has to be told everyday what to do. Yesterday you may have told him to get up, go outside and cut the grass. Tomorrow morning you have to tell him to get up and take out the garbage. The next day you have to tell him to get up and take a bath. You have to tell him what to do every single time!

Proverbs 6 communicates to the lazy person, the resourcefulness of the ant; though it has no commander, no overseer, no ruler, yet it stores up provision for summer and

gathers its food in harvest. In complete opposition to this, a lazy man lacks judgment about the seasons of his life. A sluggard does not know when his 'harvest time' has arrived, or in other words, he does not know there is a new mall going "up" down the street and that jobs are available. He has no awareness of anything; he just drifts through life oblivious to the world around him. He lacks alertness and does not even realize that the people he associates with are unhappy with him. He has no real sense of judgment in his heart.

Lazy people become tired easily and they **hate** difficult assignments. If you give them 'hard' work to do, they usually start complaining. If you start talking about working on a project, they tend to consider it too burdensome to deal with. Others around them may be working arduously, not realizing that a lazy person is in their midst who is complaining and unfairly leaving the bulk of the work for them to do.

Laziness leads to forced labor

Lazy people complain a lot. It is amazing to see how a lazy person is very critical of everything and everyone else and full of complaints: "It's too hard; I'm working too long; I don't like my boss; I don't even feel like going to work today; it's too cold; it's too hot; I'm not being paid enough," and every other reason they could think about. They are prone to not finishing their assignments on time; instead, they take longer than usual to get things done and leave a lot of unfinished tasks behind. In other words, the moment they have no supervision, they are **gone**! If there is no one to watch over them, they will not complete a task.

Lazy people procrastinate. They are always planning to do things "tomorrow" and will tell you they can get the job done at another time. It's time to stop; it's time to change.

Laziness brings on poverty. (Proverbs 10:3-4).

> "³ The LORD does not let the righteous go hungry, but he thwarts the craving of the wicked. ⁴ Lazy hands make for poverty, but diligent hands bring wealth."

Laziness invokes displeasure from an employer, as is seen Proverbs 10:26,

> "Like vinegar to the teeth and smoke to the eyes is a lazy person to his employer." (CJB)

Another version of the Bible puts it this way:

> "Having a lazy person on the job is like a mouth full of vinegar or smoke in your eyes." (CEV)

That is how an employer feels when he realizes that he has a lazy person in his employ. His perception of the lazy person can be compared to the discomfort of having your mouth gorged with vinegar or experiencing the irritation that smoke can bring to your eyes. When you have a lot of smoke in your eyes, you can hardly see where you are going. As a result, the boss may become concerned for his business and what is going to be the outcome of his livelihood with the lazy person being on the job. Not only that, but smoke in the eyes is likely to make you cry. In other words, a lazy person on the job has a 'saddening' effect on their boss, and even brings them to the point of tears. This potentially adverse

effect on their employer certainly puts the lazy person's job in jeopardy.

Laziness can stop you from fulfilling leadership positions. A lazy person will never be a good leader. Proverbs 12:24 says,

> *"Hard workers will become leaders, but those who are lazy will be slaves."* (NCV)

It does not matter where you are working, or whether they are paying you or not. Once you are on a job, give it your best shot. And always be willing to do more than what you are paid to do. That is a kingdom position. You are not working for money; work is a character issue, and it causes others to respond to you a certain way.

Diligence Breaks Through

Needless to say, a boss does not look favorably on a lazy employee; laziness stops you from attaining leadership positions and from being promoted. Laziness will hinder progress... in a man's life, in a marriage, in a church, in a corporation. 'Diligence', on the other hand, is a breakthrough component. A diligent hand will break through powerfully into abundance.

In Proverbs 15:19 the Bible says,

> *"The way of the sluggard is blocked with thorns, but the path of the upright is a highway."*

Lazy people have thorns in their way. In other words, they have a lot of obstacles.

The Bible talks about work that will bring you prosperity. There are people who are working hard but they are not breaking through to abundance because they do not know how to work smart.

Your work ethic should be determined by God and not society.

Here are some things I want you to note about work ethics:

1. Start with a vision for your life

A 'vision' or 'plan for your future' is very important. If you do not know where you are going, you will reach nowhere fast. There **must** be something in your heart that you would like to become or achieve. It is prudent of you to plan ahead. God is not against planning. In fact, it is **dangerous** not to have a vision for your life, as seen in Proverbs 29:18:

"Where there is no vision, the people perish..." (KJV)

2. Commit yourself to education

Some people ask God for things, but they don't know what to do with their lives. In other words, if you want to be a

great musician, you need to start learning music. If you want to be an architect or a designer, you need to start obtaining an education in that area. You need to know where these institutions are located, and you need to know the system to become accepted into their programs. Your mind needs to be configured with the knowledge about your future career. Take care of your own business. Adopting useful business-like strategies in various areas of your life is advisable. You need to have a set of routines. There are some things you have to do on a regular basis. And don't do them just because you feel excited about your vision. Sometimes you have to go down into a pit (so to speak) and come back out to fulfill your vision and your dream, like Joseph; but you are going to get there. Stay focused.

3. Pay attention to money

How many of you who are reading this book think that money is important in your life? How many of you think it is an important issue? The way I grew up, we were taught that 'holiness' and 'money' were in complete opposition to each other. The thinking was: once you were 'holy', you shouldn't have 'money'; and if you had 'money', it wasn't possible to be 'holy'. But even the Word of God acknowledges the importance of money. It says in Ecclesiastes 10:19 that "...money answers all things." God's Word cannot be denied,

Money should not be **'loved'** (1 Timothy 6:10), but it is an 'answer' or 'solution' to many of life's issues. Most people respond to the need for money when a financial crisis hits,

and during those tough times, that's when they become aware that they need to pay attention to this 'almost taboo' subject in Christendom. Some wait until they are getting close to retirement before they try to understand what they should do in order to have a good retirement. Most are driven by crisis and not carefully thought out financial plans for their lives. You need to have a set time where you look at personal finances. You need to know where your money is going— what are your expenses as opposed to your income? That is the first level of personal financial management, and you can devise an action plan for handling your money wisely after that fact is discovered.

4. Mind your own business

Pay attention to your financial undertakings. As you do so, you would soon realize what most of your money is being spent on; and are better able to make the necessary adjustments to curb unwise spending. But if you want to take this to another level, your work attitude must also change. Work hard; don't be lazy; be thorough; learn to complete assignments; when you start something, finish it. If you do these things, it will help you to become a better steward of the provisions God has given to you to sustain yourself and your family. Here is what the Bible says about this in 1 Thessalonians 4:11-12:

> "11-12 Stay calm; mind your own business; do your own job. You've heard all this from us before, but a reminder never hurts. We want you living in a way that will command the respect of outsiders, not lying around sponging off your friends." (MSG)

92

5. Evaluate yourself constantly or be evaluated by someone else

Ask someone to be honest with you and tell you how you are doing in the area of your spending habits. If they point out some inadequate mishandlings of your money, don't relinquish the friendship in anger and say, *"I didn't know you were thinking that way about me all the time!"* Well, you asked for it. It is actually good that you have someone to constructively critique you. A faithful friend will tell you the truth, and if the person knows you are going in the wrong direction and do not tell you anything, that person is not a true friend. The Bible says,

> *"Faithful are the wounds of a friend..."* (Proverbs 27:6 - KJV)

Practice the suggested principles and you are sure to experience a financial turn-around. Believe it or not, laziness is an issue of iniquity and it has the potential to destroy your life, therefore, it must be broken.

A diligent hand will rule, and diligent people will prosper and see the blessings of God over their lives.

Romans 12:1-2

"The way children (even adult ones) treat their parents, determines whether they offend God or not."

5

THE FIFTH HABIT THAT HINDERS

Parental Abuse

Foundation Scripture
"Honor your father and your mother, so that you may live long..."
(Exodus 20:12, NIV)

This concept of honoring or the proper treatment of parents by their children is an extremely serious matter in the sight of God. It does not have an optional ring to it, as it was permanently written in stone by the finger of God right along with the other Commandments. In fact, a promise of life and death was hinged on to this particular Commandment under the Old Covenant, and reiterated in the New as seen in Ephesians 6:1-3:

> *"¹Children, obey your parents in the Lord, for this is right. ²"***Honor your father and mother"***–which is the first commandment with a promise–* ³ *"so that it may go well with you and that you may enjoy long life on the earth." (NIV)*

'Long life' was the promised result of obeying this particular law of parental honor. The opposite of this, therefore, is also

true: the lives of children (even grown ones) could be cut short if this Commandment is not adhered to. This iniquity is not something to be taken lightly!

So, as we look at the issue of 'parental abuse', a child/person that abuses his or her parents is activating a negative law that will work against them in life, if not corrected. This law is imbedded in the universe and is guaranteed to yield its negative results upon the offenders. Often, we hear of child abuse in which a parent physically, excessively and improperly beats a child. Of course, child abuse takes on many forms, but that is not the focus of this chapter. What is material to our concern is that there are children who **do** abuse their parents and not much is said or done about it. It appears that there are very few criminal laws, if any at all, that address this matter.

Parental abuse must be of very serious concern to God, because He thought it necessary to make it a central part of the Moral Code of the Kingdom—the Ten Commandments. These were the key principles that made Israel different from all the nations around her. Remember, at that time, Israel had just come out of slavery after being in bondage to Egypt for over four hundred years. Now they were going to be a Self-Governed Nation, responsible for their own prosperity and security. God's strategy for them was to first establish a moral foundation. This is true for nations and for individuals. This Moral Code must be firmly installed in the minds and hearts of the people. It is vital, then, that we see the development of successful living begin with a set of core values as is in the Ten Commandments.

Note several things about the divine delivery of this Moral Code: At the giving of these Commandments, God manifested Himself with billowing smoke and fire, quaking mountains and other such dramatic happenings; and He did it in such a way, that the fear of God came upon the Israelites. The people were so afraid, they asked God **not** to speak to them directly, but to speak to Moses and then have Moses speak to them. Moses gave the reason why God appeared to them in such a spectacular fashion:

> [20] *Moses said to the people, "Do not be afraid. God has come to test you,* **so that the fear of God will be with you** <u>**to keep you from sinning.**</u>*"* (Exodus 20:20 - NIV)

It would also be prudent to note that right in the middle of all the hair-raising happenings, the Most High God inserted the Commandment: *"Honor your father and your mother..."* I do not believe that this was by any means coincidental. Hence, it would be safe to deduce from this that children are to be taught the fear of God so that they would take God seriously as they deal with their parents. As we see that the Commandment to treat parents correctly is imbedded in the Ten Commandments, we must realize that this is a serious matter to God and not just to parents. The way children treat their parents determines whether they offend God or not. Note as well, that there is no junior commandment or special concessions to immaturity and folly. Children (even adult ones) must treat their parents well as a way of fearing God and gaining the blessings of God. To do otherwise would create obstacles to these blessings.

The Commandments that God gave to Moses were first carved out and written by the finger of God and then handed to Moses. They were given by the pointing finger of God. Prophetically, God is pointing the way of life and success by writing with His pointing finger.

When Moses came down from the mountain and saw the disobedience of the children of Israel, he threw the God-prepared tablets of stone down on the ground and broke them. This action of 'breaking the Commandments' is loaded with powerful significance. Perhaps we may deduce from this, that some instructions which come from the hand of God can easily slip from us and, unfortunately, be broken. This is something we need to be wary of and avoid at all cost.

After the breaking of the first set of tablets by Moses, God did not leave it at that. He set about making plans to replace them. In Exodus 34:1:

> *¹ The Lord said to Moses, "Chisel out two stone tablets like the first ones, and I will write on them the words that were on the first tablets, which you broke." (NIV)*

The first set of tablets were fully prepared and written upon by the hand of God. But in order to reproduce the Ten Commandments, Moses now had to personally chisel the new tablets out of stone with his hand in preparation for the hand-writing of God. The painstaking care he must have had to do this was the action of drilling the principles into his consciousness, his sub-consciousness and into his conscience. By the time he was finished, he would have

developed the internal mechanism needed to consistently walk in the ways of God.

Take special note of the fact that the Commandments were written on 'stone'. These divine rules were not to be treated as some pragmatic idea. They were not to be that which you do when it is convenient. They were not to be kept based on the need at the moment. They were not to be ancient philosophies that changed when man became more informed or modern. They are to be engraved in stone—permanently adhered to in the fear of God. Therefore, we are to make these precepts clear to children. Children must know that they must never depart from them no matter their age or circumstances. Honoring parents is a statute of God and this ordered relationship must never be changed or redefined.

The historical configuration of the Ten Commandments was in the shape of a heart. I believe they were deliberately shaped this way to illustrate that they were not meant to be perpetually carried by physical hands, but rather, in the **heart of man**. They were not meant to be eternally stored in a box, such as in the Ark of the Covenant; they were to be carried in the heart of all mankind. They were to be a permanent systemic foundation for living. This also applies to the children of our time; they are not exempt from such a principle. As we teach them to honor, obey and treat their parents correctly, this principle is to be instilled in their hearts. To treat parents correctly must be a matter of the heart and not a matter based upon material things received from the hand of the parents.

Some parents have given everything to their children. Some have sacrificed to give children what they themselves did not have, yet many children have little care and regard for that which have come from the hand of the parents. Other parents have not been able to give children the toys and thrills that they would have preferred to have received. There are parents who raised their children in the most adverse of circumstances and gave their children little material gain and have received bitter words and attitudes from their children as a result. By their insolent responses, it is evident that the law of taking care of their parents with honor has not been written in their hearts. It is carried in their hands (in a manner of speaking) and, therefore, easily slips from them. The law of correct treatment of parents must be engraved in stone or should be a strong and abiding principle in one's heart. No person, no context, is to alter this law.

The First Commandment with Promise

It amazed me when I noticed that God attached a promise to this particular commandment of honoring your father and mother. He gave nine other commands but did not directly attach a 'promise' to any of them. He did not even attach a promise to the ones that demanded honor for **Himself**, or to avoid idolatry. But, he added the promise to **this** one. It elevates this specific commandment above all the others. It tells us how serious He takes the way children treat their parents. The way the Amplified version of the Bible renders the Ephesians representation of this verse gives us a clue as to why God did this.

100

"¹ CHILDREN, OBEY your parents in the Lord [as His representatives], for this is just and right." (Ephesians 6:1 - AMPC)

God placed a promise to correctness in treating parents well because the parents are 'God's representatives' to them. Children, we have learnt, think in concrete terms. They do not understand abstract principles as quickly as adults do. So, God chose to make parents His representatives to them. To dishonor them, then, is to dishonor God.

The promise, according to Paul, includes Long life and Prosperity when adhered to. To live long is not just a matter of good dietary or hygienic habits. It is also a matter of morality and spirituality. So is prosperity. Prosperity does not only come because of hard work and investments. Prosperity, too, comes as a result of honoring this Moral Code.

Children's Operational System - No Upgrade Available

In the computer environment, Operating Systems are central to the functioning of the computer. In graphical terms, the Operating System is the 'house' in which everything on your computer works. It is the main program that tells your computer how to execute the commands of the end-user, or how all the devices added are to be used. Every other program lives inside of the Operating System. Among the modern ones are Windows 10 for PCs. At the writing of this book, MacOs Mojave 10.14 is the most recent Operating System for Macs. The more modern ones are most effective.

In the Kingdom of God, 'Obedience' and 'Honor' are the permanent Operating System, so to speak, and is so advanced that it needs no Upgrade. There is no upgrade available for them. Also, they cannot be hacked or corrupted. There is no known virus to penetrate them.

What I mean is: 'Honor' and 'Obedience' describe the Operating System of children. All of their inner devices and functions come out of these two most powerful positions. Children are to be wired with these principles. Let's take another look at Ephesians 6:1-3:

> "¹ CHILDREN, OBEY your parents in the Lord [as His representatives], for this is just and right. ²HONOR (esteem and value as precious) your father and your mother—this is the first commandment with a promise—[Exodus 20:12]. ³ That all may be well with you and that you may live long on the earth." (AMPC)

'Obedience' is **foundational** to a child's attitude towards his or her parents. Several things are implied. First, there is faith. To 'obey' or to 'carry out a parent's orders' is to 'believe' that the parent has the child's best interest at heart and wants them to succeed when an instruction is given. Next, it indicates that the child is on the parent's side in the general moral issues of life. The idea of obedience is not just that the child is doing what the parents say, when they say it, but are responding to the good intentions of the parents even when the word is not spoken. The child is to come on to the side of the parents, or, as we sometimes say, *"be on the same page."*

To obey, by virtue of its literal definition, carries the idea of listening to the instruction and holding it dear to one's heart so as not to forget. It implies that sometimes 'forgetting' is a moral flaw. Sometimes 'forgetting' is the result of not paying attention to, or, slighting what the parent is saying.

'Honor' or 'holding one's parents in high esteem', on the other hand, can be compared to the Operating System in the computer world, from the standpoint of what is called the 'control panel' in Windows. In the 'control panel' of the Windows Operating System, there are several applets or small programs that allow the end-user to configure some of the workings of the Operating System without damaging it. This is vitally important, since laws are inadequate to address **all** circumstances which may occur from time to time. When honor, like love, is present, it will guide the child to know what to do when a 'written' command is not present that is applicable to the new situation regarding their parents.

This is why honor appears not to have practical demonstrations when it is mentioned. The Bible simply says that a child is to honor its parents. I heard someone say that honor is 'manifested respect'. This is true. We may say then, *"Children,* **respect** *your parents!"* Yet this is still abstract. God knows that every situation is different, and every family and parent would have its individual nuances. But when respect is present, correct behavior is inevitable. To honor is to value. To honor parents is to value them. Value is based upon benefits and consequences. Value is based upon need as well. Children NEED parents. Their parents brought them into the world when they could have aborted them. A parent can abort the

103

life of a child while in the womb; but by mistreatment, can abort the destiny, progress, success or prosperity of the child. A parent can either provoke the blessing of God on a child or curse them. This power is not given to the peers of the child, but to the authority figures, namely, the parents.

Therefore, the child is to treat the parents with immense value. This value is ever permanent and never ceases. God demands it and blesses because of it.

'Honoring' is as perennial as the grass. It is a basic and vital foundational position to face life with. No one is to hold the place of a parent in a person's life. A man can have several 'women' but can have only one biological father and one biological mother.

The words of Adam in his joyous astonishment in seeing this new creature (the woman) which he had never seen before, is not an absolute doctrinal position as he could not speak on matters of love or honor of parents since he had never had one. Genesis 2:24 says:

> "²⁴ *For this reason a man shall leave his father and his mother and shall be joined to his wife; and they shall become one flesh.*" (AMP)

This verse and the three subsequent references to this passage do not point to the '**abandonment** of parents' but, rather, to the '**permanence** of marriage'. (Matthew 19:5; 1 Corinthians 6:16; and Ephesians 5:31-33). The marriage is not to be the end of parental honor. To leave them carries the idea of ceasing to receive physical and emotional care from them.

In some cases, it requires that the new couple be physically removed from the home of the parents to provide a brand-new context for raising the newly formed family. In **no way** does it mean that when two persons become married that they should 'abandon' their parents.

Watch It Children

Springing out from this law, we see throughout the Bible, a number of warnings to children as they relate to their parents. Let's peer into some of them:

1. **A child should never be violent towards his or her parents.** This means they should avoid fits of rage, physical aggression, or angry body language.

   Exodus 21:15 says:

   "15 Anyone who attacks their father or mother is to be put to death." (NIV)

   I like the way the Message version puts it:

   "15 If someone hits father or mother, the penalty is death." (MSG)

2. **A child should not verbally abuse their parents.** They should not raise their voice (yell) at them. They should not say things to their parents that hurt their feelings. They should not use profanity at them.

Exodus 21:17 makes this abundantly clear:

"¹⁷ Anyone who curses their father or mother is to be put to death." (NIV)

3. **Children should not begin scandals on their parents.** They should not take the private knowledge of the failures of parents and irresponsibly scandalize their name. An example of this can be found in Genesis 9:20-25:

"²⁰ Noah, a man of the soil, proceeded to plant a vineyard. ²¹ When he drank some of its wine, he became drunk and lay uncovered inside his tent. ²² Ham, the father of Canaan, saw his father's nakedness and told his two brothers outside. ²³ But Shem and Japheth took a garment and laid it across their shoulders; then they walked in backward and covered their father's naked body. Their faces were turned the other way so that they would not see their father naked.
²⁴ When Noah awoke from his wine and found out what his youngest son had done to him, ²⁵ he said,
"Cursed be Canaan!
    The lowest of slaves
    will he be to his brothers." (NIV)

The Bible does not elaborate on the failure of Noah, nor does it pronounce a judgement from God upon him for what he did. But it elaborates on the seriousness of Ham's behavior. Ham's

discreditable behavior brought irreparable harm to his son, Canaan, as a result of what he did to his father, Noah. For many years I was unsure as to what Ham did to provoke God's disfavor until I looked at the verb 'to tell' used to describe Ham's report to his brothers on the failure of his father. The word in Hebrew is 'nagad', [pronounced 'nawgad']. It carries the idea of exposing, scandalizing, expounding, and elaborating or predicting an outcome. He was responding in a scandalous way when he got information that his father did something wrong.

4. **Children should not ignore parents when they are addressing them.** They should ensure that they answer the phone when they call. When parents are addressing their children, they should stop speaking and give their father or mother their undivided attention. These are the emblems of honor and value.

   Proverbs 23:22 states:

   "*22 Listen to your father, who gave you life, and do not despise your mother when she is old.*" (NIV)

5. **Children should not abandon or ignore parents.** Let's look at The Message version of Proverbs 23:22:

"22 Listen with respect to the father who raised you, and when your mother grows old, don't neglect her." (MSG)

6. **Children should not react negatively to the disciplinary measures of Parents** but should respond correctly. This has all kinds of implications. When parents set the rules for the conduct of the family, children should respond with a good heart. As an example, they should carry out the instructions given to them by their parents regarding chores. They should not sneak people into the house unknown to their parents. They should not look at XXX movies in the house, or smoke cigarettes or marijuana, nor participate in any other forbidden practices either. Rules are put in place for a reason, and parents usually have the child's best interest at heart when implementing same. Therefore, children should avoid despising their parents for any disciplinary measures taken when these rules are broken.

Proverbs 15:5 says it this way:

"5 Only a fool despises a parent's discipline; whoever learns from correction is wise." (NLT)

Let's look at Proverbs 15:5-6 in The Message version of the Bible:

"⁵ Moral dropouts won't listen to their elders; welcoming correction is a mark of good sense. ⁶ The lives of God-loyal people flourish; a misspent life is soon bankrupt." (MSG)

7. **Children are not to shame the family name:** Since the parents are to represent God to the children, this verse found in Leviticus 22:32 can be applied:

"³² Do not bring shame on my holy name..." (NLT)

Children are to ensure that by their words and attitudes, they do not shame the family name. They should not allow anyone to look shamefully on the legacy of their parents. Instead, they should seek to make others honor their parents by the way they conduct themselves.

Practical Guidelines for Honoring Parents

1. **Make an early decision to serve the Lord.** This does not even need a scriptural reference to establish it. Nothing brings joy to a parent like a child who walks with God. Even when the parent is unsaveåd and unchurched, most of them feel a sense of bliss to look upon a child that is serious in their faith in Christ. Children should honor God first and love Him with all their heart and all their soul and all their mind.

This has promises attached to it; not just for this life, but for the afterlife. It is a comforting thing, especially for Christian parents, to know that they will spend eternity in Heaven with their children.

Parents are delighted to hear children pray, or to see them actively involved in worship. It brings joy when children are tithing and involved in the service of the Kingdom of God. Not only does that please God, but it brings great satisfaction to their parents' heart.

2. **Socialize correctly.** Nothing hurts a parent like seeing a child descending into a sub-culture of degradation. I have seen the pain of parents when their children are hanging with the wrong crowd. When children are spending prolonged periods of time with drug addicts; drug abusers; violent, unproductive and poorly dressed company; the concerned parent knows that this spells trouble. Proverbs 1:10 expresses a word of caution:

"10 My son, if sinful men entice you, do not give in to them." (NIV)

A child should be a leader and not just one that follows along with others. I have heard this saying possibly over a million times in my youth: *"Show me the company you keep, and I will*

tell you who you are." The choice of company speaks to your values. If the child is not like their current company as yet, it is more likely than not that the child would end up with similar values as the company that he or she is keeping.

3. **Give back to your Parents.** In times past, when our parents were growing up, the systems of social security, pension or other Governmental programs that provided for the elderly were not available. So, successful children were, in a sense, a retirement plan—providing for their elderly parents. The Apostle Paul also encouraged this benevolent practice in 1 Timothy 5:4:

    "⁴ But if a widow has children or grandchildren, these should learn first of all to put their religion into practice by caring for their own family and so repaying their parents and grandparents, for this is pleasing to God." (NIV)

    The Apostle Paul treats this proposition as a requirement of God. (It pleases Him.) The Apostle Paul regards the care of parents and grandparents as if it is the responsibility of their children and grandchildren. In cases where they are negligent or absent, then the Church should take up the responsibility.

111

The scriptures treat this too as if it is an economic obligation. Note that it says, *"...and so **repaying** their parents and grandparents."*

4. **Marry good spouses.** Proverbs 31:2-3 states:

    "² O my son, O son of my womb, O son of my vows, ³ Do not give your strength to women, nor your ways to that which ruins kings." (NET)

In the above text, the mother is pleading with her son to avoid women who would sap his strength from him and bring him to ruin. Instead, from verses 10 to 31 of the same chapter, she describes the alternative virtues of a wife of noble character whose value is far above rubies; a choice that would be much more beneficial to him.

However, it is important to note that while it would be ideal for parents to approve of their child's choice for a spouse, a child is not obligated to marry the person their parents love, as *they* are the ones that must live with the person all the days of their life. Equally, parents should not demand or put pressure on their children to marry the person that they (the parents) prefer.

With that being said, it is usually very important to parents that their child enters into a successful marriage. This begins with choosing wisely, which may involve heeding the wise counsel

of their parents. Almost every parent's hope is that their children marry spouses that will help them to succeed at their life's assignment; and avoid mates that squander substance and is lazy or violent.

5. **Be affectionate towards them.** Bowels of compassion and sensitive care are important in the Kingdom of God. One should be gentle and kind to all mankind. If this is so, then we may apply it to parents as well. Attitudes of affection and words of kindness are vitally important to parents. Children should speak in a loving tone of voice. They should touch their parents affectionately. Give them the seat of honor. Take them to and from events and to and from appointments when they are unable to go themselves. Children should ensure that their parents are in a safe and healthy environment. Loving, compassionate treatment of one's parents is strongly advised. To treat them adversely, whether this means lashing out at them physically or with negative words, is sure to block your blessings and bring about detrimental repercussions. Proverbs 19:26-27 cautions against parental abuse:

"26 Kids who lash out against their parents are an embarrassment and disgrace. 27 If you quit listening, dear child, and strike off on your own, you'll soon be out of your depth." (MSG)

Proverbs 30:17 concurs:

"¹⁷ An eye that disdains a father and despises a mother—that eye will be plucked out by wild vultures and consumed by young eagles." (MSG)

6. **Excel in the area of your Education.** Proverbs 10:1 puts it this way:

*"¹ ...A **wise** son brings joy to his father, but a foolish son brings grief to his mother."* (NIV)

In another place we see:

*"¹¹ Be **wise**, my son, and bring joy to my heart; then I can answer anyone who treats me with contempt."* (Proverbs 27:11 – NIV)

In both scriptures we see that when a child acquires wisdom, it brings honor and joy to the parents. It would not violate the text to establish that a child should seek to succeed with formal education.

In our culture, this means that one should successfully complete a high school education and move on to higher levels of learning. A child dishonors parents by being a drop-out or by failing courses due to negligence. Children should be aware of the joy they bring to their parents when they are well learnt, not just formally, but that they live in a wise and prudent way.

7. **Children should not steal from Parents**. The Amplified version of the Bible puts this point found in Proverbs 28:24, in an amazingly accurate way.

    "²⁴ *Whoever robs his father or his mother and says, This is no sin—he is in the same class as [an open, lawless robber and] a destroyer.*" (AMP)

    God is displeased when a child embezzles or irresponsibly disposes of the material substance of a parent. We may apply this in many ways. For example, when a child wastes money, food, or utilities, it is displeasing to the Lord. Children should avoid wastage and abuse of the resources in a home, whether the parents are wealthy or not. We used to say that, "*a willful waste will bring a woeful want.*"

8. **Obey them**. Once again, we do not even need to quote the Bible to establish the legitimacy of obedience. Although this principle is modified by Maturity, Marriage and Mission from God, it is critical. The word used for "leaving" parents when getting married is not just applicable to the marriage situation. It means to '*loosen the grip*'. When one becomes married, he must loosen the grip that parents have over his life. This should also be applied when a child is growing up. The more mature

the child becomes, the strength of instructions from their parents increasingly loosens. This is true when the child is grown and married and/or has a legitimate call from God on his or her life. We can see this in the life of the Lord Jesus. In Luke 2:49, He appears to be blunt about being about His Father's business (God's) when addressing His earthly parents, Mary and Joseph, about the reason for His disappearance. He eventually submitted to their authority, but by His actions, it was obvious that His 'grip' on them had been 'loosened'.

However, within reasonable age limits (and we are not able to specify as it varies), children should follow the advice and instructions of parents. They should have a high respect for them and live as close as possible to their best values.

This list is by no means exhaustive. There are many other areas where children can honor their parents. I attempted to touch some of the critical areas for general guidance. I must emphasize, though, that the benefits gained are greater to the child than to the parent. For the most part, the parent has already lived most, if not all, of their lives. The child is facing their future. When they treat their parents well, the forces of Heaven back them up. Help comes from God and favor to give them access to opportunities and success. God has promised the child who honors their parents and treats them well, a good long life and prosperity.

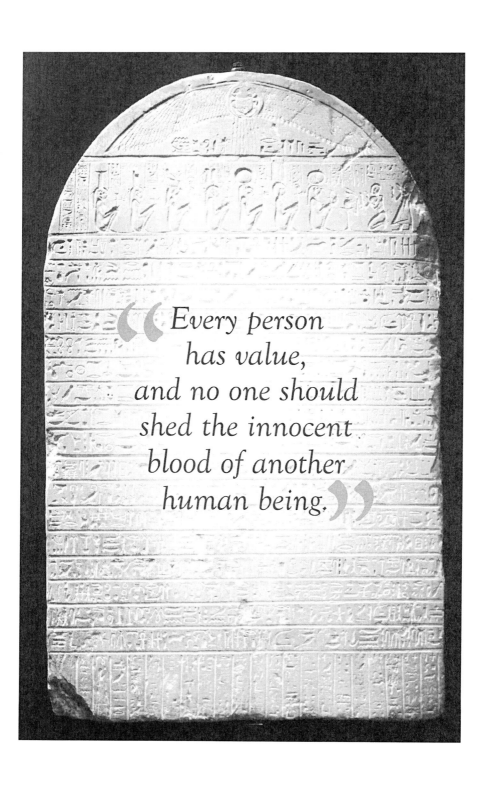

"Every person has value, and no one should shed the innocent blood of another human being."

6

Taking Human Life Through Murder

Foundation Scripture
"You shall not murder."
(Exodus 20:13, NIV)

The creation of mankind was not an 'afterthought'. God articulately and purposefully designed and made 'man' in **His** image.

The Word of God says: *"...God created man in His own image, in the image of God He created them; male and female He created them,"* (Genesis 1:27).

We have been His prized possessions since the beginning of time.

The fact that God made us in His image emphasizes the critical **value** of the human being to God, and this value must be upheld in our relationship with each other. Every person has value, and no one should shed the blood of another human being, as is plainly communicated in the Scriptures:

"Whoever sheds the blood of man, by man shall his blood be shed; for God made man in his own image." (Genesis 9:6 - ESV).

Though this should not be done, a *distorted* view of humanity has made it easier for one person to take the life of another through murder.

I need to provide clarity here on the subject of '**killing**' vs. '**murder**'. Some Bible versions of Exodus 20:13 say, *"You shall not* **kill**," but a more accurate translation of the Hebrew is, *"You shall not* **murder**."

There are some forms of killings that are justified by God, such as in the case of war. There are also justifications to kill in the line of protection of self or family from someone who attempts to harm you. The Bible and the law of the land sanction killings by a civilian under certain circumstances.

However, one is forbidden to **murder**, i.e., **wrongfully** take someone's life. Capital punishment is also a legal course to rid the society of criminals. God *does* permit the penalty of death on the one who violated His law by taking the life of someone. However, God's deterrence is against **murder**.

Murder is the illicit taking of an individual's life. This must be underscored! Murder as it is understood, deals with the **intentional** slaying of another person. God *does* make allowances for accidents or unintentional loss of life, but for the **deliberate** act of killing another, His response to such is DEATH!

I heard a story about an old man who fell sick while driving and could not lift his foot off the accelerator. As a result, he ran his car into a crowd of people, killing four persons. This unfortunate incident happened because the old man had a stroke. Accidents such as these are not considered murder!

In Israel, God commanded the Jews to establish seven cities of refuge for persons who may have killed someone by accident. Any person who may have caused the death of another accidentally was urged to run to one of those cities for refuge. If they arrived before the avenger caught them, then they had a chance of having their life spared. These are the provisions God made for the unintentional killing of another human being (Joshua chapter 20).

Love as a Principle vs. Murder as an Outcome

Now, you could imagine how serious this is to the heart of God! It is said that the average person, 15 years old in America, has seen about 16,000 murders on television. As a consequence, the human spirit is becoming callous, and the life of others is being taken for granted and regarded as being almost valueless.

Long ago in St. Vincent and the Grenadines, my country of birth, a murder would enrage the **whole** country. There was a silence that came over the whole land when someone was murdered.

It is sad to see how human beings have lost the value of their own species. To love another becomes the highest priority in life. It keeps the order of God. The Bible urges us to "Love one another," (John 13:34-35).

The most valuable thing in the world is not gold or silver, but human life.

The Bible also speaks of the bowel of compassion, mercy, love, and affection for the brethren. It says in Romans 12:10,

> *"Be devoted to one another in love. Honor one another above yourself."*

Additionally, the Scriptures say in Ephesians 4:32,

> *"Be kind and compassionate to one another, forgiving each other, just as in Christ God forgave you."*

Cursed is the Land because of Murder

Whenever innocent blood is shed, the land becomes cursed. The shedding of innocent blood curses a community. Deuteronomy chapter 21 reveals how Israel had to seek atonement for the death on an individual. From verses 1-9, the

Scriptures tell us what steps were to be taken if an individual was found dead in a field and the murderer was unknown. The village nearest the field had to break the neck of a special heifer; the elders of that village were to assemble and wash their hands over the heifer, whose neck was broken, and declare their innocence. This act purged the people from the guilt of the shedding of innocent blood.

From all indications, bloodshed defiles or pollutes the land, and God holds the people and their territory guilty for the death or murder of an innocent person. Therefore, when someone is murdered, it is a very serious offense in the sight of God and the result is a curse on the land. God warns His people saying:

> *"Do not defile the land where you live..."* (Numbers 35:34a)

Consequently, murder hinders the blessings when innocent blood is shed. God urges us to uphold justice. In our civilized community, a person accused of murder is arrested, tried before a court of law, and if found guilty, that person may be sentenced to death or imprisoned for a specific duration based on the judge's ruling and the various appeal processes.

In Deuteronomy Chapter 27, there are laws given by the Lord governing human relations:

> *"24Cursed is anyone who kills their neighbor secretly...*
> *25Cursed is anyone who accepts a bribe to kill an innocent person...*
> *26Cursed is anyone who does not uphold the words of this law by carrying them out..."*

We must not tolerate violence and murder. In the New Testament, Jesus Christ enlarged the discussion on murder by saying: *Raca- Empty head, Stupid, blockhead*

> "²¹You have heard that it was said to the people long ago, 'You shall not murder, and anyone who murders will be subject to judgment.' ²²But I tell you that anyone who is angry with a brother or sister will be subject to judgment. Again, anyone who says to a brother or sister, 'Raca,' is answerable to the court. And anyone who says, 'You fool!' will be in danger of the fire of hell." (Matthew 5:21-22)

If you are in a state of prolonged anger against anyone, you could be hurting yourself. It could become easy to retaliate against the person responsible for the anger, and may result in you physically hurting the individual, the object or source of your anger.

If murder stops your blessing and the root of murder is anger, then living in anger is blocking the flow of God's blessing in your life. When a man or woman is angry, it can lead to taking the life of another, and sorrow follows. You can hit a person in anger, not intending to commit murder, but your actions could result in fatally causing harm. God deals with anger the same the way He deals with murder. That's why God says to settle disputes quickly:

> "²⁶In your anger do not sin. Do not let the sun go down while you are still angry, ²⁷ and do not give the devil a foothold." (Ephesians 4:26-27)

This means your anger should last only for a brief moment. There are some people who are angry for years; and to some extent, their anger results in bad health. You ought not to be angry for days, weeks, months, years... In the eyes of God, you are as guilty as the murderer.

Get Rid of Anger... Foster Blessings

Furthermore, living with unforgiveness, quarrelling, and bitterness could be harmful to your relationship with God Himself. Indeed, your relationship with others can be affected, but more importantly, your relationship with God could be severed.

Because anger is a force that promotes violence to others, murder, or some kind of physical abuse, it will serve as a hindrance to your blessing and your success. We take these things lightly, but it is true. Anger can be demonstrated in road rage, animal cruelty, spousal abuse, child abuse, neglect of chores, responsibilities, and the like.

God wants to give you a continuous flow of blessings. That is why He talks about having His rivers of living water flowing within you to help you through your crises...

> "37...Jesus stood and said in a loud voice, "Let anyone who is thirsty come to me and drink. 38 Whoever believes in me, as Scripture has said, rivers of living water will flow from within them." (John 7:37-38)

Do not give anybody the privilege of hindering your blessings by harboring uncontrolled anger against them. It's not worth it!

The Bible talks about unresolved anger, that is, anger at a level that cannot be entreated; no one can calm you and you are not prepared to discuss anything. God expects us to settle the matter quickly; sit down and deal with it, as angry as you are! Furthermore, the Lord instructs us in Matthew 5:23-24, that if you bring your offering to the altar and you remember that someone has an issue with you, leave the offering; first go and discuss your problem with the person who may have something against you, and **THEN** come and offer your gift to Him.

> *"23 Therefore, if you are offering your gift at the altar and there remember that your brother or sister has something against you, 24 leave your gift there in front of the altar. First go and be reconciled to them; then come and offer your gift."*

This is a necessary step toward removing anger and setting yourself on a path to living with the joy of the Lord and having His peace in your heart.

Uncontrollable anger is sin.

Love as an Instrument over Anger

In addition, the Scripture extols the virtues of love. Not being easily angered is one of those virtues. First Corinthians 13:4-5 stresses that:

> *"⁴ Love is patient, love is kind. It does not envy, it does not boast, it is not proud. ⁵ It does not dishonor others, it is not self-seeking, it is not easily angered, it keeps no record of wrongs."*

You must care enough to release the offenses of another, show kindness, and let love govern your conduct in every situation so that anger will not have a "strong hold" in your life.

Controlled anger is an act of love.

Remember, *"Love never fails..."* (1 Corinthians 13:8). On the other hand, murder defiles the land! It is more advantageous to love than to remain angry with another. Forgiveness is the key to avoiding this particular iniquity.

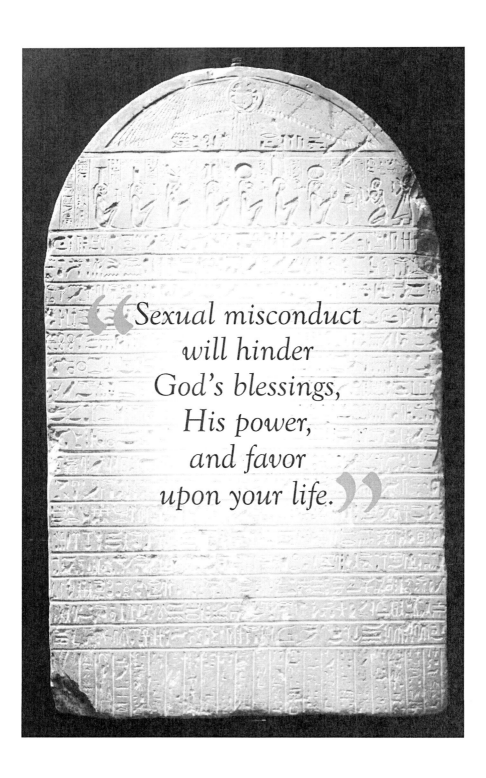

"Sexual misconduct
will hinder
God's blessings,
His power,
and favor
upon your life."

7

THE SEVENTH HABIT THAT HINDERS

Sexual Misconduct

Foundation Scripture
"You shall not commit adultery."
(Exodus 20:13, NIV)

L et us examine the iniquity of 'adultery' also known as the iniquity of 'sexual immorality'. In Exodus 20:14, God commands us not to commit adultery. Adultery is voluntary sexual intercourse between a married person and a person who is not his or her spouse; or any sexual relation with the spouse of another person. This act is viewed as iniquity in the sight of God.

In the Bible, adultery was regarded as a great social wrong, as well as a great sin. The Mosaic Law (Numbers 5:11-31) prescribed that a wife suspected of committing adultery should be tried by the ordeal of the "water of jealousy." There is, however, no recorded instance of the application of this law. In subsequent times, the Rabbis made various regulations with the view of discovering the guilty party, and of bringing about a divorce. It has been inferred from John 8:1-11 that this sin became very common during the age preceding the destruction of Jerusalem.

Adultery will hinder God's blessings, His power, and favor upon your life.

But adultery is more than just an 'act'. This iniquity took on a whole new dimension when the Lord Jesus also included the lustful 'yearning of one's heart' as also being considered 'adulterous' in its intent. Matthew 5:27-28 says:

> "*27...You shall not commit adultery. 28 But I tell you that anyone who* **looks at a woman lustfully** *has* **already** *committed* **adultery** *with her* **in his heart.**"

So, adultery can also be lustful matters of the heart. The Bible uses the word "adultery" not just to speak of sexual relations with the spouse of another person, but to speak of and deal with **every** form of sexual immorality.

There are commandments concerning various forms of iniquitous behavior that were written on the tablets of stone, but under this new dispensation, the Bible says in 2 Corinthians 3:6 that we are not following those laws exactly as they are written (the 'letter' of the law), but we are now governed by the 'spirit' of that law (a spiritual perspective). To make this a little clearer, let's say one is accused of committing adultery, one might say in response to the accusation that, "I did not have sexual relations with the man," or "I did not have sexual relations with the woman," to justify their actions. But they were pecking, necking, kissing, and only stopped at the point of sexual penetration. Jesus is saying here, that even

if you did not have penetration, from Heaven's perspective, you still violated the commandment regarding adultery.

When God commands us not to commit adultery, He is not just talking about sexual penetration; it is about **everything** that accompanies the issue of immorality.

So, what does it mean to be moral? The word 'moral' deals with 'good standards, good behavior, good attitude, and good conduct'. Webster's dictionary uses standards for a principled person, as being a person who practices things that are good.

Sexual Immorality

An 'immoral' person is the opposite of someone who has 'good' standards. It is a person who practices 'bad' standards and makes iniquitous, morally wrong choices. God warns us about being immoral. A person can be immoral in many areas, but the Bible also warns us about 'sexual' immorality. That means there are bad standards being displayed in the area of 'sexuality'.

In 1 Thessalonians 4:3-8, the Word of God says:

> *"³It is God's will that you should be sanctified: that you should avoid sexual immorality; ⁴that each of you should learn to control your own body in a way that is holy and honorable, ⁵not in passionate lust like the pagans, who do not know God; ⁶and that in this matter no one should wrong or take advantage of a brother or sister. The Lord will punish all those*

who commit such sins, as we told you and warned you before. ⁷For God did not call us to be impure, but to live a holy life. ⁸Therefore, anyone who rejects this instruction does not reject a human being but God, the very God who gives you his Holy Spirit."

We often hear sermons about material prosperity and God's plans to bless us, but we do not want to get blessed in the way the world does it. Many think they are blessed because they won the lottery or through other 'get-rich-quick' schemes such as gambling. To walk in the abundance of God requires that you walk in the utmost integrity. God wants you to avoid sexual immorality in any manner thereof.

- **Lust**

   The commandment about adultery also means you must refrain from every kind of sexual immorality, including 'lust'. Lust is in effect when a person desires to have unlawful sexual relations with another that is prohibited. It is when someone yearns to be affectionate with another person in an illegitimate manner. A wife should crave after her husband and a husband should long for his wife, and no other.

   Lust is a sinful longing; the inward sin which leads to the falling away from God (Romans 1:21). Lust is the origin of sin, and it has its place in a person's heart. In Mark 4:19, 'lusts' are objects of desire. It is associated with adultery, greed, incest, lasciviousness, sensuality, and

sodomy. Lust is an **abnormal** appetite in a worldly manner.

Fornication

Fornication is voluntary sexual intercourse between persons not married to each other; also falling into the category of 'extra-marital sex' or 'free love'. We are to avoid fornication at all cost. The Apostle Paul sternly warns us in 1 Corinthians 6:18 to...

"18 Flee from sexual immorality [fornication]. All other sins a person commits are outside the body, but whoever sins sexually, sins against their own body."

While we must strive to avoid **every** kind of sinful act, we are specifically told to **FLEE** from fornication or sexual immorality. To **'flee'** is to **'run away from a place or situation of danger'**. The severity of this particular sin is viewed differently by God as it involves sinning against our own bodies (the temple of the Holy Spirit). Fornication and every other form of sexual immorality is not something to be tampered with, experimented with, or played with. We are told to **"RUN!"** when faced with this iniquitous temptation.

Each of these sinful acts serves as open doors for the enemy to come in and block the blessings that God has for your life. You must be determined to live a holy life, be a pure vessel of honor in the eyes of God, so that the favor of God will never be held back from overtaking you in every aspect of your being—physically, socially, emotionally, financially, educationally, and all other areas of your life. The blessings are yours, but you must be willing to turn your back on the iniquity of committing adultery, fornication, and every other act that is reprehensible in the sight of God. Let's look at some of the terms used to describe various forms of sexual misconduct:

- **Adultery.** The Bible is replete with counsel against adultery. It strongly promotes sexual fidelity within the bonds of marriage. Here is the apostle Paul's guidance found in 1 Corinthians 7:1-5

   "¹ Now, getting down to the questions you asked in your letter to me. First, Is it a good thing to have sexual relations? ² Certainly – but only within a certain context. It's good for a man to have a wife, and for a woman to have a husband. Sexual drives are strong, but marriage is strong enough to contain them and provide for a balanced and fulfilling sexual life in a world of sexual disorder. ³ The marriage bed must be a place of mutuality – the husband seeking to satisfy his wife, the wife seeking to satisfy her husband. ⁴Marriage is not a place to "stand up for your rights." Marriage is a decision to serve the other, whether in bed or out. ⁵Abstaining from sex is permissible for a period of time if you both agree to it, and if it's for the purposes of prayer and fasting – but only for such times. Then come back together again. Satan has an ingenious way of tempting us when we least expect it." (MSG)

- **Incest** is treated as a wrong way to obtain sexual fulfillment within the family structure and falls within the judgmental disposition of God.

  "22 Cursed is the man who sleeps with his sister, the daughter of his father or the daughter of his mother." Then all the people shall say, "Amen!"

  "23 Cursed is the man who sleeps with his mother-in-law."
  Then all the people shall say, "Amen!"
  (Deuteronomy 27:22-23 - NIV)

- **Rape** is forced sexual relations. A person is not allowed to force sex on another or manipulate someone to obtain sexual fulfillment.

- **Masturbation:** This may fall into the category of lust. It is not an area of sexual behavior upon which we can dogmatically say is evil.

- **Petting:** One should not be engaged in these sexual gestures without being married to the person to whom this form of affection is directed. The fondling of the private parts arouses sexual desire, and when not practiced within the confines of marriage, it provokes lust, and so becomes sin.

- **Bestiality:** Sexual relations with an animal is strongly prohibited by God.

"²¹ Cursed is anyone who has sexual relations with any animal."

Then all the people shall say, "Amen!"
(Deuteronomy 27:21 - NIV)

- **Homosexuality and lesbianism:** These terms refer to males and females who have sexual relations with someone of the **same** gender. There is an abundant supply of biblical teachings that makes it very clear that God does not sanction homosexuality. By the destruction of Sodom and Gomorrah, we see God's disposition against such behavior. Romans 1:26-27 also reveals how this act is viewed by Heaven as defilement:

*"²⁶ Worse followed. Refusing to know God, they soon didn't know how to be human either – women didn't know how to be women, men didn't know how to be men. ²⁷ Sexually confused, they abused and **defiled** one another, women with women, men with men – all lust, no love. And then they paid for it, oh, how they paid for it – emptied of God and love, godless and loveless wretches."* (MSG)

- **Necrophilia:** Necrophilia is a sin! It is the act of sexual relations with a corpse. This is clearly wrong, though there is no real clear treatment of the subject in any passage. Sex belongs in the bonds of marriage. When that person dies, God permits remarriage. This is to demonstrate

that we are not allowed to continue sexual relations with that person in their dead state.

- **Orgies:** An orgy is a group people engaging in open sexual relations or engaged in any open sexual activity and vulgarity.

- **Pornography:** This is the root concept of fornication. It is looking with gratification upon others in sexual relations via printed or visual forms. Billions of dollars are made each year through this avenue. The internet is loaded with sites where pornography is free or easy to obtain. This is clearly wrong as well.

It is important to note how the Lord puts the curse as a consequence to these kinds of misconduct. It is the reason why we say that they block your success and your prosperity. The curse is an invisible barrier to the fortunes of life. This kind of behavior literally makes the forces of the environment revolt against you. In the book of Genesis, it states that thorns and thistles would grow up and work against you and hinder your crops from growing or hinder you from reaping the crops. The 'thorns' are anything in the material environment, even people, that work against you. Then it says that by the sweat of your brow you will eat bread. This means that to succeed would be harder when these kinds of behavior exist in your life.

It is evident that the environment has been instructed by God to negatively respond to any person who does not comply with the will and the purposes of God. Creation is groaning and waiting for humanity to act like God. It is waiting for the uncompromising 'sons of God' to arise and deliver it from its state of ruin.

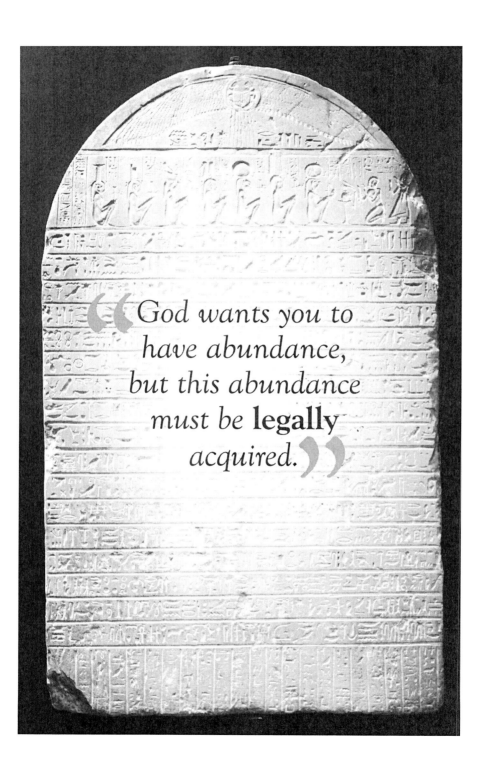

"God wants you to have abundance, but this abundance must be **legally** acquired."

8

THE EIGHTH HABIT THAT HINDERS

Stealing

Foundation Scripture
"You shall not steal."
(Exodus 20:15, NIV)

Iniquity is a habit or a pre-disposition to a particular sin. Wherever you go, even if you change your location, change your clothes, your house, friends; who you are will eventually show up because it is rooted inside of you. It's called a 'fault'.

A scientific definition for 'fault' is a crack beneath the earth's surface indicating that there is a problem. It has a geographical accent to it, and it has the ability to shift any minute and probably create an earthquake.

In life, a 'fault' means there is a problem beneath the surface of **who you are**! For example, if you stole when you worked at a certain store in another country and you get the same kind of job elsewhere dealing with money, you are more than likely to start stealing again. In other words, it would not be long before that 'fault' shows up again.

The bad habit of 'stealing' has the ability to block the power of God to prosper you. Exodus 20:15 says, *"You shall not steal."* This law is about prosperity and your well-being.

When you understand **why** God gives certain instructions, it becomes easier to walk in obedience. The Ten Commandments is an economic framework. The only nation other than the Jews in the history of the world that built its sense of nationhood on the Ten Commandments is the United States. It became an economic giant since Egypt and Assyria, Rome, Greece, the Medes, the Persians and even the Empire of Communism.

Covetousness will destroy an economy.

Today the economy of the United States is still one of the most powerful economies in the history of the world. This is so, because inside the Ten Commandments there is more than just an intrinsic value for prosperity and obedience to God.

- When God says you shall not covet your neighbor's house, that is an economic principle.

- Secondly, the Bible says six days you shall labor and rest for one day; that is an economic law. Not only is the day of the Sabbath that God instituted, critical, but the day of rest to the well-being of a nation.

If you have people working a full day for six days, you have a tremendous economic environment. The Ten Commandments were not only provided to keep you from sinning, but also to provide the infrastructure for you to build enormous prosperity.

The command, *"You shall not steal"* is to prevent the **unlawful** acquisition of substance. God wants you to have abundance, but this abundance must be **legally** acquired and protected from thieves, bandits, robbers and extortionists. One would assume that after accepting Jesus Christ you would know **not** to steal. However, some Christians *do* steal, but should not!

I once visited a city where I received my first laptop from someone there. Two weeks later, the man was arrested for pilfering laptops from his job. He was a thief!... and he was caught by the authorities! Stealing has consequences.

Some people steal money. Some may take other things that do not belong to them. Some people think that because they do not feel any pain as an immediate aftermath of their thievery, God is not judging them. The primary judgment of God is forfeiture, meaning that you do not initially realize what you are missing.

When Adam and Eve sinned, God removed them from the Garden. They forfeited a place of abundance. He denied privileges from them because of their stealing habit (taking of the fruit that did not belong to them).

There are some people who steal intellectual property. For example, they might sing another person's song or poem and pretend it's their own. They may not realize that is stealing, but it is! People can also steal another person's opportunity. Let's say I have money that I want to give to a specific person; someone might say to me **that** person doesn't need anything, then they will begin telling me about their **own** needs in order to re-direct the blessing. That is thievery of a favorable moment that is designated for someone else.

In the high-tech era in which we live, we now have what is called 'identity' thieves. These are people who fraudulently steal your private identifying information such as your Social Security Number and pretend to be you. This crime is usually committed for financial gain and making unauthorized purchases. It is an evil iniquity to pretend to be someone else.

There is another area of theft called 'stealing a person's heart'. It can also be referred to as the workings of the 'Absalom spirit', and it is devilish in its operations. Its aim is to turn the loyalties of people's hearts away from one, unto themselves. Absalom, King David's son, was one such person through whom this spirit operated (hence the name). In 2 Samuel chapter 15, we get a peek into the workings of the Absalom spirit and how it 'steals people's hearts':

"*¹In the course of time, Absalom provided himself with a chariot and horses and with fifty men to run ahead of him. ² He would get up early and stand by the side of the road leading to the city gate. Whenever anyone came with a complaint to be placed before the king for a decision, Absalom would call out to him, "What town are you from?" He would answer, "Your servant is from one of the tribes of Israel." ³Then Absalom would say to him, "Look, your claims are valid and proper, but there is no representative of the king to hear you." ⁴ And Absalom would add, "If only I were appointed judge in the land! Then everyone who has a complaint or case could come to <u>me</u> and <u>I</u> would see that they receive justice.*"

⁵Also, whenever anyone approached him to bow down before him, Absalom would reach out his hand, take hold of him and kiss him. ⁶ Absalom behaved in this way toward all the Israelites who came to the king asking for justice, and so <u>he stole the hearts of the people</u> of Israel."

Before Absalom's intervention, the people had been faithfully going up to David for counsel and aid, and they were loyal to him as their king. However, Absalom positioned himself in a way to circumvent the people's loyalty to his father and began promising to provide them with better solutions to their problems. By doing this, he succeeded in stealing the people's hearts away from King David, to such an extent that the king had to FLEE from his kingdom! Stealing another's heart is an extremely wicked thing to do.

The Absalom spirit can also be present in a church. If someone is fond of a particular person, others may become jealous and start defaming the favored person, whilst pretending to be more advantageous to be associated with. Consequently, people begin to give their loyalties to that person. When Absalom stole the hearts of the people, he robbed someone of the love and commitment of other people. That is a form of theft that is very dangerous. We may not think that it is important, but God watches these things. Absalom, David's son, paid dearly for this crime.

Another form of 'stealing' can be found in the workplace. When you work for a boss who is paying you for a day's work and you slack off all day, you are stealing from your boss. When you are being paid for work you have not done, it is theft.

God wants you to work for more money than people pay you. That's a kingdom principle.

Always work for more money than your salary.

If you are looking for God to bless you, a good habit to develop is to work for more money than you are paid. If they

tell you to go a mile, go **two** miles! Do not steal. When you are unsupervised, you should ensure that there is integrity in your heart; and work as if your boss is watching you.

If you do well only when you are supervised, then you are a people-pleaser, ungodly, and exemplifying iniquity. People like that will never progress in life. I am telling you these things because most people want the blessings, but they are not prepared to get rid of the iniquitous behavior that blocks the blessings. Right living attracts the prosperity of God from a kingdom standpoint, whilst iniquity repels it.

The Bible says in Matthew 6:33 to seek first the Kingdom of God and His way of doing things and all other things will be added unto you. Look for God's way of doing things and watch His blessings come upon your life.

An important point to note is that not only do some 'employees' steal. The flip side to stealing on the job can be when 'employers' work their employees laboriously and do not pay them adequately for their work. That employer is 'stealing' from the employee. If you own a business and have people working for you, it is important that you pay them well.

Another thing that is considered stealing is when you destroy other people's property. For example, if someone loans you a tape recorder and you give it back totally broken: that's stealing. When someone loans you a book and you return it in a torn-up condition, that's stealing. Reckless destruction of property is theft. When God issued the command that we are "not to steal", one of His intentions was to protect people's property and the things that they have built.

Forging other people's signatures is another example of stealing. And anytime you keep your tithe, you are stealing from God. This is the worst kind of thief. A person who steals from God will steal from anybody. Can a man rob God? Is it possible to steal from God? Yes! When you withhold your tithe, you are stealing from God.

In order to get rid of this problem of theft, there are some things you need to learn:

- How to live in contentment.
- How to walk in the power of contentment.

Greed may lead people to steal things, especially when they are trying to keep up with the social status of others. They might look at another person in a nice suit, and because they are impressed with how that person is dressed, they start desiring what the other person is wearing for themselves. They might even be best friends with the person and feel that because the person got a new suit, they should have one too. However, they may not even know how their friend got the suit in the first place. But eventually, because of greed, some begin doing compromising things they should not do in order to get what someone else has.

Learn how to be content. Contentment is the ability to exist in unfavorable circumstances and not stoop to ungodly behavior. Even if you have a need and you are tempted to steal, a contented person won't fall prey to the temptation. You will learn how to exist in your situation despite what you have need of.

I sometimes remember the days when I had very little. I know what it is to live in a house without a refrigerator. When my aunt bought her refrigerator, I felt important. I told everyone around that we had a refrigerator. I would walk by the refrigerator very frequently and open it, though it only had one bottle of water and some ice in it. I would curiously open it to see if the ice was freezing.

My brother and I grew up in a house, where there was no running water in the pipes. We had to travel great distances to get water and bring it into the yard to fill up a barrel. We used water from that barrel to wash our hands and face. Life was tough, but we enjoyed it. We didn't know a better life and we didn't know a better way. When we went to school, we only had two white shirts to wear while most of the other children had six or seven. We would wear one, wash it and put it behind the refrigerator to dry.

We sometimes ran around the yard with our bare feet through the grass that contained pieces of broken bottles and other sharp objects. As a result, we sustained numerous cuts and bruises under our feet. I couldn't go to my mother and tell her I wanted a pair of tennis shoes, because I would be punished. I learned to be content in whatever state I was in. Kids today do not know anything about being content. One example is of a young girl who nagged her mother for a pair of tennis shoes and because she didn't get them, she hung herself. Another example is when a girl jumped onto the train tracks because her cell phone fell, and she wanted to get it back.

The apostle Paul said he **learned** to be content in whatever state he was in.

> *"12 I know what it is to be in need, and I know what it is to have plenty. I have learned the secret of being content in any and every situation, whether well fed or hungry, whether living in plenty or in want."* (Philippians 4:12 - NIV)

Though my siblings and I didn't have a whole lot when we were growing up, we didn't steal from our neighbors. We didn't jump their fence and steal clothes off the line or run off with other children's toys. We learned how to live with the little we had and thank God for it.

Contentment is a powerful source. It's an integrity issue.

Proverbs 16:8 says,

> *"Better a little with righteousness than much gain with injustice."*

The Amplified Bible says,

> *"Better is a little with righteousness."*

In other words, it's better to be righteous with little, than to be unrighteous with much. Keep the righteousness of God in your heart, and He will come through for you. Philippians chapter 4:10-13 teaches us to be content, whatever our circumstances. When you are content, you will not steal.

Contentment comes from intimacy with God that draws strength from His Presence.

Contentment is a God-given grace. Most people interpret Philippians 4:13, *"I can do all things through Christ,"* to mean that they can fly an airplane or succeed at doing this or that. But Paul was specifically talking here about his ability to exist in a state of contentedness and peace **while** having needs. So, when you say that you can do all things through Christ who strengthens you, it is implying that you may not have much, but you can still be godly and do what is right.

If you are filled on the inside with the presence of the Lord, there is fullness of joy in your heart and at His right hand there are pleasures forevermore. If you are living in the light of the presence of God, you should not be frustrated by the fact that you did not get a new suit this year; but rather, your

demeanor ought to be one of contentment. Adopting this attitude ensures that you can stand in the midst of your lack.

Now the other dimension that cures theft is when you learn not to make the mistakes of the poor. Ephesians 4:28 says:

> "²⁸ Anyone who has been stealing must steal no longer, but must work, doing something useful with their own hands, that they may have something to share with those in need." (NIV)

Remember, if you are completely fulfilled in your pursuit of happiness and prosperity, you do not have time to steal from others. Here are five mistakes that the poor make which hinder them from coming into abundance:

1. They are secured with a salary

The average poor man is content to live from one stream of income. One profound error that many people make is choosing to live on one salary.

Ecclesiastes chapter 11:1-2 advises us of a more prudent way to live. It says:

> "¹ Cast your bread upon the waters, For you will find it after many days." (NKJV)

> "² Invest what you have in several different businesses [Give a portion to seven, even eight], because you don't know what disasters [evil] might happen [occur in the land]." (EXB)

When we are told to "Cast our bread upon the waters," it means "to give"; but we are also advised to make **multiple** investments in life, for we do not know which one will come back successfully. When you are operating on this level, you do not have time to steal. You are excited about building an empire for yourself because this is the will of God. The Living Bible (TLB) puts it this way:

> "*¹Give generously, for your gifts will return to you later. ²Divide your gifts among many, for in the days ahead you yourself may need much help.³When the clouds are heavy, the rains come down; when a tree falls, whether south or north, the die is cast, for there it lies. ⁴ If you wait for perfect conditions, you will never get anything done.*" (Ecclesiastes 11:1-4)

Most people are waiting until they have it all together, then they would invest; but the lesson we can learn from this portion of scripture is: do not wait for everything to be perfect before you invest elsewhere. If you are waiting for the conditions to be perfect, you will **never** get anything done.

Do not depend on one harvest or on one salary. If that income stops for some unforeseen reason, then you will encounter financial difficulty. It is advisable to have more than one stream of income.

Bishop TD Jakes says, "*Nobody in the world, who works for people for a salary all their life, builds prosperity.*" You will never really come into abundance if you trust your job to pay your salary. This is why some people resort to stealing from their employers.

2. They believe a Formal Education is enough to bring prosperity

There are many *poor* educated people. I absolutely advocate getting an education, but it is also extremely important to develop your knowledge of finance and business. I often meet frustrated people who hold Masters' degrees, but who are not prospering.

In his book, *"Rich Dad, Poor Dad,"* Robert Kiyosaki talks about the two fathers he had in his life. One was educated and worked for the government. This one got a loan and bought a house and worked all his days to retirement, but generally could not enjoy abundance. The other 'Dad' was the blood father of his friend, and so Robert was able to access the life and culture of a father who built prosperity. This one was not really formally educated, and he did not carry many degrees, but was a businessman who became highly prosperous and successful.

The poor makes this unprecedented error in thinking that they need a degree from a college to obtain success in life. Nothing can be further from the truth. In today's world knowledge is everywhere. For the most part, leaders are looking for people with the core competencies to fit a job opportunity, and not just those who possess certificates.

3. The poor and the needy prefer a home before business

Acquiring a home of your own is referred to as the 'American Dream' which pushes the idea that everyone should rush to

154

buy a house. People will go to the bank and obtain a 30-year mortgage; though they're building equity, the house can become an obstacle. People will work for years to pay off the mortgage and end up paying several hundred thousand dollars in interest. Additionally, they have to deal with taxes. The lender wants to know everything about you and what assets you own. The system indicates they're not going any further than the house they bought. To go further, they will need a lender. But this rush to purchase a house before being economically solid is not a biblical concept. Proverbs 24:27 says:

> "[Put first things first.] Prepare your work outside and get it ready for yourself in the field; and afterward build your house and establish a home." (AMPC)

In other words, it is prudent of us to get a business, develop an enterprise, and have that functioning first before purchasing a home.

The Living Bible puts it this way,

> "Develop your business first before building your house."

God's people should be an enterprising people.

4. The poor and the needy do not see the need for a financial mentor

You need a mentor. You need someone who is qualified to show you how to handle your financial matters effectively. Not acquiring a financial mentor is the mistake of this age, and

God is concerned that many of us do not have wealthy and successful friends to show us the way. People need someone to look up to in the natural. You must be willing to submit to a mentor to realize there is someone who has gone ahead of you that you can learn from. You have to acknowledge greatness when you meet it. You must acknowledge someone who is stronger and wiser than you; and be humble enough to ask them to teach you how to make improvements and adjustments where it is necessary.

There is so much pride in people's hearts that many do not want to submit themselves to others for help, though they may have been working for many years and have nothing to show for it. Some *want* to save but are unable to. Their lifestyle is beyond their income. At some point, they must become brutally honest with themselves, and be willing to sit with someone and acknowledge they need to be taught how to increase financially.

You have to find a mentor, even if that person is not present in your generation. You could draw from someone who has already died by reading their writings or by studying their life. You can have a mentor that is older or younger than you. Age doesn't matter; once the person is stronger in the area you need to enhance, that is the important thing. And when you identify your mentor, you have to be the one to pursue that person. That is wisdom for living. A mentor does not chase a protégé or the mentee. The 'mentee' has to pursue the 'mentor'.

One example of this mentoring relationship is found in 2 Kings chapter 2 with Elijah and Elisha. Elijah was busy

fulfilling the purposes of God when Elisha started pursuing him. Elisha was so adamant about following Elijah, that not even Elijah's protests were able to stop him from doing so. Elisha said to his mentor, *"As surely as the Lord lives and as you live, I will not leave you."* Elisha's persistence was tested on several occasions, but he stuck it out until the mantle of his 'mentor' Elijah was eventually passed down to him.

A 'disciple' is a 'disciplined follower'. Disciples are made by others. You have to allow someone to 'make you', so to speak. You must be open for a candid evaluation and straight talk.

5. The poor and the needy generally possess a bad attitude towards money

Some people have a bad attitude towards money. If you have a bad attitude as it relates to money, you will chase it from you. You must have a new attitude about money, as you attract the things you like. You have to realize it is good to have wealth, and that it is in the will of God for you to do so. Many of the poor trapped in a lifestyle of poverty have stopped believing that they can do better financially. Many people do not realize the foundation of success and the prosperity of God is locked into their 'belief system'. Some do not even believe they **deserve** to prosper.

The thing you dislike, you will never attract.

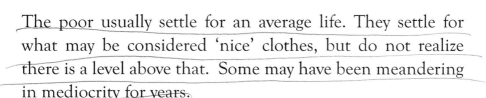

The poor usually settle for an average life. They settle for what may be considered 'nice' clothes, but do not realize there is a level above that. Some may have been meandering in mediocrity for years.

There is something called 'excellence' which should be considered when making purchases. For example, instead of buying 4 or 5 different pairs of shoes of low quality, you can buy one good pair that will last a long time if you take care of them.

'Excellence' is a beautiful thing, but most people settle for 'average'. This 'settling' is a mistake many of the poor make, and they do not realize that by embracing an indifferent position, it results in creating liabilities in their lives. You should take your time to acquire excellence.

The children of God must believe they are royalty. I believe His Highness deserves our best, which is exemplified in a spirit of excellence. You must strive to take upon yourself a disposition of excellence. Your choices must be excellent; the way you speak must be excellent; and there must be excellence even in the way you handle your finances. Excellence in the area of your finances puts you in the position to lend and not borrow. God wants you to have enough to give to others and still have enough to spare. That is God's will for His children.

God expects you to have so much, that 'stealing' would not be a part of your vocabulary. You do not have to live in greed, nor covet other people's things. Those attitudes will destroy you. If you receive the abundance of God, your life goes to

another level. Let us examine 2 Corinthians chapter 8 verse 9. It says,

> *"For you know the grace of our Lord Jesus Christ, that though he was rich, yet for your sake he became poor, so that you through his poverty* **might become rich.**"

From this verse of Scripture, it is so abundantly clear that God wants you rich. In the same way Jesus took stripes on His body for your sickness, and you can boldly say you are healed, He also took your poverty, so you can be rich. It's all part of God's plan; in fact, it is God's **Covenant**. It doesn't matter what you 'physically' have right now; **you are rich!**

Two people in a ditch cannot help one another. God keeps somebody outside the ditch to help the one who is down in the ditch. Proverbs 13:22 says:

> *"A good person leaves an inheritance for their children's children, but a sinner's wealth is stored up for the righteous."* (NIV)

The wealth of the wicked is laid up for the righteous. God is transferring wealth into the hands of His people. When you lift your hands to Him, they are not empty. You lift your hands because God is blessing you. You are stretching your hands for the provision of God. He does not want you to fall behind in any good thing. God wants you to have enough to spare. He wants you to labor with your hands so that you can have something to give to someone else. God wants you to have all the redemptive provisions of Christ. However, the

act of 'stealing' blocks up these redemptive provisions and prevent them from getting to us.

In this discourse, we are not suggesting that only the poor have a problem with theft. Stealing is not just a matter of external stimulation, but it is a character flaw that both the rich and the poor experience.

The rich tend to steal in more sophisticated ways. They create unjust financial products that trick others and swindle their money. They create unjust laws, raking in millions from the unsuspecting poor. The rich manipulate legal and political systems. They institute unjust taxation systems that favor the very wealthy. Recently I learnt that that the Amazon corporations paid no federal tax for the fiscal year of 2018. This is one of the richest and most powerful companies in the world. I am not necessarily against that; what I am saying is that the system must be just towards all. The rich certainly rule over the poor in every culture and in every nation.

God warns us about the iniquity of stealing because it is a dangerous practice. I adjure you—whether rich or poor—do not steal from anyone, because when you rob others, God will withhold from you.

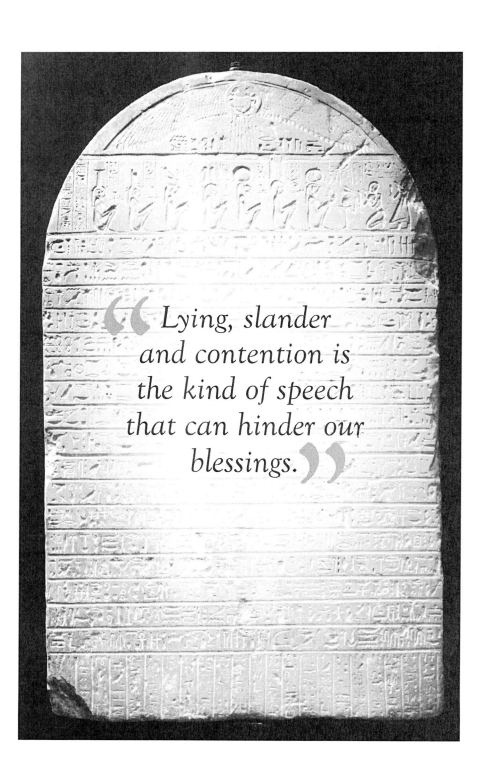

Lying, slander and contention is the kind of speech that can hinder our blessings.

9

The Ninth Habit That Hinders

Lying

Foundation Scripture
"You shall not give false testimony against your neighbour."
(Exodus 20:16, NIV)

The Ten Commandments serve as a guide in our daily living. They are not burdensome nor grievous. The Commandments of God instruct us to avoid iniquities because they will block the blessings of God. Now in Exodus 20 verse 16, the Bible says you shall not give false witness against your neighbors. We are dealing specifically here with the iniquity of lying, slander and contention— the kind of speech that can hinder our blessings.

There are several forms of lying. We may hide behind the subtler forms of falsehood, but it is still treated as being untrue and, therefore, evil in the sight of God. Some forms of lying include:

1. **Misstating facts.** There are people who knowingly misstate information. Sometimes it is used to gain an unfair advantage over one

163

considered to be a rival. Other times, it is done to produce harm.

2. **Deceit:** A person can tell a story which is intended to give another person the wrong impression about a matter. A brother once came to my house and told an amazing story about himself and a televangelist as though they were best of friends. Then he implied gross sexual immorality on the part of the preacher. It turned out that he did not have the facts but painted a picture of proximity with the preacher to validate what he was saying. His picture of proximity to the preacher was intended to deceive me into thinking that because he was close, he had the facts. This is a problem of deceit.

3. **Exaggeration:** Exaggeration is the act of saying more than is necessary. The statement includes truth, but truth that is amplified. The Bible teaches us, "let your yea be yea and your nay be nay." Then it says all else proceeds out of evil.

4. **White lies:** White lies are lies told in jest, or a lie about a matter considered insignificant.

5. **Plagiarism:** People sometimes take the intellectual property of others and treat it as their own and use it to gain wealth or some social advantage. This is lying, and it is also theft.

We are warned about speaking words that falsely accuse or defame the character of our neighbors, because the words we speak are very powerful. Proverbs 18:21 tells us:

> *"The tongue has the power of life and death, and those who love it will eat its fruit."*

God is telling us a man's mouth can release death forces. That is why we must speak the **right** words over our children and our church. We must be careful, because we can speak words that will destroy them and our relationships with them. Our mouth can ruin our marriages. It can ruin personal relationships and cause us to lose our jobs. Our mouth can also give us ulcers and other diseases.

The Bible is a manual. It is a manufacturer's instructions on how to use a product. An airplane has a manual. When pilots sit in the cockpit, they refer to their manual to tell them how to fly the plane; how to manipulate the laws of gravity; how to bank to the left and the right; how to navigate the plane. In order for us to understand how human beings operate, we must go back to our manual; the Bible is God's manual. Our manual says our mouth can kill us. It says if we do not know how to use our lips and tongue in a useful way, it can literally destroy us. On the other hand, our mouth can bring us blessings and prosperity. Now it's not just what we say, but also what other people say about us that could be a curse or a blessing.

Words can create death forces, and poverty is a death force. Sickness and disease are death forces. Death forces can cause accidents and mishaps. Our mouth can destroy or heal our bodies. It can destroy or heal marriages and relationships.

There is a story in 2 Kings chapter 5 about an army commander named Naaman and the prophet Elisha. Naaman came to Elisha with leprosy and was healed. Naaman wanted to bless the prophet with some gifts out of gratitude, but the prophet did not accept anything from him so Naaman left with his gifts. Gehazi, Elisha's servant, ran after Naaman concerning the blessing. Naaman was a wealthy Syrian General, and when Gehazi saw what this man was carrying to bless the prophet of God, he just did not think the man of God should refuse to accept it. So, he slipped out the back door and went and told Naaman a concocted story and Naaman gave Gehazi the blessing. After this act of dishonesty, Gehazi went back to the house and stood before Elisha, his master, who asked,

> [25b]"Where have you been, Gehazi?"
> "Your servant didn't go anywhere," Gehazi answered.
> [26] But Elisha said to him, "Was not my spirit with you when the man got down from his chariot to meet you? Is this the time to take money or to accept clothes—or olive groves and vineyards, or flocks and herds, or male and female slaves? [27] Naaman's leprosy will cling to you and to your descendants forever."
> (2 Kings 5:25b-27)

As recompense for Gehazi's underhandedness and falsehood, the prophet told him that Naaman's leprosy would cling to him and his descendants forever. Then Gehazi went from Elisha's presence and he was leprous, as white as snow. The

prophet Elisha told Gehazi that this disease would come on him and he and all his children would die—this was a generational curse—and it happened just as he said. Life and death are, indeed, in the power of the tongue!

In Joshua 6:26 we see another example of the power of the spoken word. The Bible says that Joshua pronounced a solemn oath:

> *"Cursed before the Lord is the one who undertakes to rebuild this city, Jericho: "At the cost of his firstborn son will he lay its foundations; at the cost of his youngest will he set up its gates."*

What Joshua said is, after Jericho was destroyed, anybody who tried to rebuild Jericho city would do so at the death of their firstborn and youngest son. Five hundred years later a man tried, as recorded in 1 Kings 16:34:

> *"³⁴ In Ahab's time, Hiel of Bethel rebuilt Jericho. He laid its foundations at the cost of his firstborn son Abiram, and he set up its gates at the cost of his youngest son Segub, in accordance with the word of the Lord spoken by Joshua son of Nun."*

Just as Joshua had spoken so many years prior, when Hiel rebuilt Jericho, he really did so at the cost of the lives of his firstborn and youngest sons. After all those years, Joshua may have been forgotten, but what he decreed came to pass!

Words are important, and if we are to break into 'God-promised' prosperity, we must be careful as to how we speak about other people. We are told not to falsely accuse or speak

negative words over other people's lives; and even our own life.

In Genesis chapter 27, Rebekah said, *"Let the curse rest on me."* By saying this, she pronounced a curse upon herself in place of her son, Jacob, when she prompted him to deceive his father Isaac for the birthright. So, our words can bless people and our words can curse other people. Our words can also bless us as well as curse us. When we say we are under a curse, we are inviting a curse. When we say we are so stupid, then we are encouraging stupidity into our own minds. Some people say they will never live to be over 50 years. When we say that, our words are destroying our future because words have power to it.

The iniquity of hurting other people's lives with words can hinder your prosperity. You must speak words of blessings over your life. It does not matter how difficult the situation you may be in, you must be able to say, **"I will prosper."** You may be sick, but by Jesus' stripes you are healed. Learn to speak words of victory, words of success, and words of prosperity. Do not bow under pressure; use your words and turn your life around.

Always say what God says about you. God says you are blessed. God says all your needs are met. He says you are more than a conqueror. And if the doctor gives you a bad report, you must choose whose report you will believe: the report of the Lord, that you are **healed** by the stripes of Jesus!

You must be careful with people who slander others and are contentious. People who have no control over their words may justify their actions by saying, *"Well, it's the truth!"* Slanderous persons may speak what is true, but with a **bad** spirit, and **dangerous** motives.

Again, I remind you, God's Word says you should not bear false witness. This directive is not just referring to speaking the truth when you are in a court of law, but also includes how one is to speak about others in general. A person who bears false witness is someone who hinders the blessings of God in the lives of others, and ultimately upon their own lives, because whatever you sow in life, you **reap!**

Your harvest is always bigger than your seed!

Slander is anything communicated to others that reduces the value of another person. If, for example, I am saying something to somebody about another person, and when I am done, the person I just spoke to is looking down on the person we were having a conversation about, then I reduced their value in that person's heart.

The Bible gives a strict command about slander, and I want you to see this. In Leviticus chapter 19, verse 16, it says,

> *"Do not go about spreading slander among your people."*

What you say can be endangering. It may not kill the person *physically*, but you could spoil their lifestyle or mar their reputation. Do not go about spreading slander or defaming another person's character. Now, a slanderous person's spirit is very 'dry', and does not know the presence of God. I do not care how spiritual they may **sound**; they might say, *"Praise the Lord! Hallelujah!"* but I can guarantee you, someone who has a slanderous habit has a dry spirit, and their spirit man is weak and powerless.

Psalm 15:1 says,

> *"Lord, who may dwell in your sacred tent? Who may live on your holy mountain?*

... That is the presence of God.

Who are the ones who will have the presence of God working in their heart, and the blessings and favor of God over their lives?

> *"The one whose walk is blameless, who does what is righteous, who speaks the truth from their heart;* **whose tongue utters no slander..."**

A slanderous person hurts others, and it is iniquity! David was privy the damage that slander can bring about in a person's life. His agony was expressed in Psalm 31:10-13a:

> *"¹⁰ My life is consumed by anguish and my years by groaning; my strength fails because of my affliction and my bones grow weak. ¹¹Because of all my enemies, I am the utter contempt of my neighbors, and an object of dread to my closest friends—those who see me on the*

street flee from me. *12 I am forgotten as though I were dead; I have become like broken pottery...*(NIV)

*13a...***For I hear the slander of many.***" (NKJV)

David said his bones hurt; they were weak; and he was in anguish of spirit. Slander can affect someone so deeply that it creates pain in their spirit, and even impact them physically.

In Psalm 41:6 David gives some more insight into his experiences with the distresses of slander and falsehood:

> "*6 When one of them comes to see me, he speaks falsely, while his heart gathers slander; then he goes and spreads it around.*"

In other words, he was saying, "*When the person came to me, he came speaking falsely, but when he spoke falsely he was listening for what I would say. When I began to speak, he was gathering more slander, then he goes out and spread, not what he brought, but what he had just gathered.*" Brand new, juicy news!

The iniquity of slander and false accusations are, for the most part, ignored and not dealt with as sin, but in the eyes of Heaven, it has all the markings of being 'wicked'! It defiles and makes one 'unclean'.

Jesus said in Mark 7:20-22,

> "*20 The things that come out of a man are the things that make him* **unclean.**" (ICB)

> "*21 For it is from within, out of a person's heart, that evil thoughts come—sexual immorality, theft, murder,*

[22] *adultery, greed, malice, deceit, lewdness, envy, slander, arrogance and folly."* (NIV)

But, thankfully, there is hope for those of us guilty of slander and any of the other listed sins. Ephesians 4:31 says, **"Get rid of all** bitterness, rage and anger, brawling and **slander..."** In other words, it's not over. Whatever the situation, whatever the iniquity, if God said **get rid of it**, then you can **stop it**! I want you to know that God doesn't love you any less. Some churches make the mistake of ostracizing a person because of a moral failure or iniquity in their lives. God does not respond that way. In fact, the Word of God says, *"...the* **goodness** *of God* **leads** *you* **to repentance**.*"* (Romans 2:4 NKJV).

God cares about you, and you can still experience the abundance of divine provision. He has not changed His mind about blessing you because you have a habit of slandering—or any iniquity for that matter. He still wants to, and is eagerly yearning, to get His heavenly supply to you. But He KNOWS that iniquity presents a hindrance to these blessings, hence, He gives the instruction to stop! He is not saying this in an accusative manner. God truly wants to help you break the hold of that iniquity on your life and desires that you respond in humility and contrition of heart so that you can be washed clean.

Say this prayer of repentance:

> *"God, I know that this is an area I've messed up in; I have not been able to handle getting information about others without spreading it abroad; I have not been responsible with the things that I hear. God, help me to overcome in this area, in Jesus' name."*

Submit yourself to the workings of the Holy Spirit in your heart and believe for your cleansing. In 1 John 1:9, the Word of God says,

> *"If we confess our sins, he is faithful and just to forgive us our sins, and to cleanse us from all unrighteousness."* (KJV)

We are not under condemnation when we stand under the blood of Jesus Christ. The thing that most Christians have not learned as yet, is that God truly loves them. The thing we have not fully comprehended as yet is though we were all guilty, we have been justified; that is, declared or made righteous in the sight of God!

Another aspect of iniquity is a 'contentious' person: one who is a disagreeable person; always in disagreement. They hardly walk in agreement with anyone. They are self-opinionated and conceited. It is hard for them to submit to somebody else's ideas. A contentious person is always trying to prove themselves as being right.

A contentious person violates the law and the power of agreement. That is why we have to be careful. The people we share our dreams with must be people who are willing to agree with us. We need the power of agreement.

No devil could handle us when we are united.

The devil cannot handle God's people when we are united, because unity is seen in the supernatural realm like the 'anointing'. Psalm 133:1-3 shows how unity sets the 'good' and 'pleasant' atmosphere for the anointing to flow and for the blessings of God to be lavished upon His people.

> *"¹ How* **good** *and* **pleasant** *it is when God's people live together in* **unity***!*
> *² It is like precious* **oil** *poured on the head,*
>   *running down on the beard,*
> *running down on Aaron's beard,*
>   *down on the collar of his robe.*
> *³ It is as if the dew of Hermon*
>   *were falling on Mount Zion.*
> *For* **there** *the Lord bestows his* **blessing***, even life forevermore."* (Psalm 133:1-3 - NIV)

A contentious or quarrelsome person works against unity by destroying the power of agreement. They engender division among a people group—whether in a nation, in a church, on the job, or in a home, thus weakening its foundation. Jesus made it clear in Mark 3:25 that *"If* **a house is divided** *against itself, that house* **cannot stand.***"*

The spirit of discord, when it is sown, has the potential to take root in someone's heart and blossom into heated disagreements and prolonged conflicts. A contentious spirit can sabotage the move of God, and even detract from your faith. You have to be careful not to give in to the assaults of a contentious spirit.

We are admonished in 1 Thessalonians 4:11 to, *"...make it your ambition to live quietly and peacefully, and to mind your own affairs and work with your hands, just as we directed you."* (AMP)

It is God's will that we all live quiet and peaceable lives; not lives filled with contentions, quarrels and disagreements with others. We are not to falsely accuse another person. This type of behavior falls into the category of 'iniquity'! You must make sincere efforts to remove the things that are blocking your breakthrough; and get rid of everything out of your life that would hinder the flow of God from gaining access to you, for this is well-pleasing in His sight.

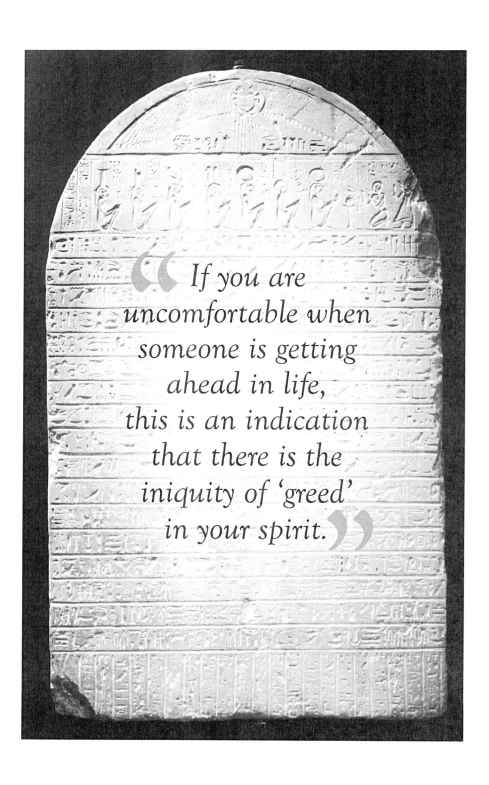

> *If you are uncomfortable when someone is getting ahead in life, this is an indication that there is the iniquity of 'greed' in your spirit.*

THE TENTH HABIT THAT HINDERS

Greed

Foundation Scripture

*"You shall not covet your neighbor's house. You shall not covet your
neighbor's wife, or his male or female servant, his ox or donkey, or
anything that belongs to your neighbor."*
(Exodus 20:17, NIV)

Another bad habit or iniquity we are admonished
about is what the Bible calls 'covetousness', better
known as 'greed'. To 'covet' is to have a strong desire
or yearn deeply to possess or have something that **belongs to
another.**

Deuteronomy 5:21 says,

> *"You **shall not covet** your neighbor's wife. You **shall
> not set your desire** on your neighbor's house or
> land, his male or female servant, his ox or donkey, or
> <u>anything</u> that belongs to your neighbor."*

In this particular verse, God deals with His dislike for
'covetousness' or 'greed' in a person's life. As powerful and
omnipotent as God is, 'greed' can block the power of God

177

from working in your life. The Word of God instructs us that we should not covet...or be greedy. God is warning you and me that if we step into these conditions, we will not maximize His power on our lives. To come into great prosperity, it is imperative that we break all these habits. There is a family of words associated with greed that we are going to look at:

- **Covetousness:**

    When the Bible says, *"Thou shall not covet,"* it means "don't be greedy." 'Covetousness' and 'greed' are the same.

- **Lust or Avarice:**

    When you hear of someone being avaricious, it means that they are greedy. These words refer to having a strong desire and an intense craving for a thing. Is God against desire? No! But He is simply cautioning us about the 'object' of the desire. In order for a desire to be qualified as being lewd, we must have certain 'unlawful' things added to this desire. For example, God says do **not** desire **your neighbor's wife**; don't desire **your neighbor's house, land, ox, donkey, man-** or **maid-servant** etc. We are not to have a strong desire or yearn deeply to possess or have something that **belongs to another**.

God is not against desires that are pure. For instance, God wants you to have ambition and He wants to give you the things you desire. In fact, the Word of God says in Psalm 37:4,

"Delight yourself also in the Lord, and He shall give you the desires of your heart."

He also promises us that, *"...**whatsoever** you **desire** when you pray, believe that you receive it and you shall have it."* (Mark 11:24).

In 1 Timothy chapter 3 verse 1, Paul assures us that, *"If a man desires the office of a bishop,* **he desires a <u>good</u> thing.**" So, God is clearly not against 'desire' per se. You can have an ambition for success, and it is allowable for you to want **'things'** because God says, "what **'things so ever'** <u>you</u> desire when you pray...." It is acceptable to desire a car; it is alright to desire a house—just as long as the 'thing' you desire is not your neighbor's or in the possession of another person. It is permissible to desire a wife or a husband, as long as they do not belong to someone else. In order for the 'desire' to fall into the category of 'greed' or 'covetousness', it means that the 'desire' has taken on a quality that is off-limits! I want to show you what 'greed' really is.

Greed exists when you are discomforted by the success of others.

A greedy person does not like it when someone else appears to be successful. For example, if you look at what your neighbor has achieved, and you cannot celebrate their accomplishments with them, greed is existing in your spirit. In other words, you do not like to see someone else prosper; and that characteristic gives way to 'malice' or 'evil intentions'. The language that 'greed' speaks sounds something like this: *"I want that thing that you have; but as long as you have it, I won't be happy with you!"*

179

You must **celebrate** the success of other people. If you are uncomfortable when someone is getting ahead in life, you have to be careful. This is an indication that there is iniquity in your spirit. You must understand that God knows what is going on in your heart, and that is a deciding factor as to whether the blessings of God can flow freely to you or be restrained from getting to you. You may find that your life is not breaking out and flourishing as you would like, and this may be because there are iniquities concealed within the recesses of your heart that are blocking your pathway.

Greed is present when you make a commitment to dispossess other people of what they have. There are some people who may lie about someone or magnify their errors because they want the person to lose their position on the job. They may even go as far as accusing the person of 'kissing up to the boss' for some kind of gain.

A greedy person will say and do anything to deprive someone of what they have. This is why when you are getting ahead in life, you must allow 'God' to be the One blessing you, because whom God bless, no man can curse. Promotion comes from the Lord; it doesn't come from the East, it doesn't come from the West, it doesn't come from the North or South; promotion comes from the Lord. (Psalm 75:5)

Greed becomes evident when you are unwilling to share your possessions. Remember, it is okay for us to 'desire', but for 'desire' to be called 'greed', all these other negative components fit into it. Greed is an unwillingness to share.

The Bible gives a parable of a man in Luke chapter 12, whose barns brought forth a lot, and the man stood up and said (paraphrased), *"Hahahahaha, look at me now. Praise the Lord! Look at how blessed I am. He said, 'I will tell my soul take it easy now, and I could spend the rest of my days in ease. I will build up my barns and store up everything that I have.'"* And the Bible said that God showed up and penalized him for his greed because he was not rich towards God.

I remember some years ago when I attended college, a few of the other students (who were also preachers) demonstrated a high level of greed. My friends and I would be in the dorms for the weekend and be forced to **'fast'**, not because we loved God, but because **we had nothing to eat**! Some of our fellow-students, though they knew our plight, would lock themselves up in their rooms with a lavish array of food, whilst their brothers were on the outside starving, and would not offer us anything to alleviate our hunger. It's funny now, but it was not then. Their unwillingness to share with us falls into the category of 'greed'.

God sometimes tests us by presenting us with the opportunities to share with others in need. Our response determines whether we pass or fail this test. True prosperity in our lives will come when we can freely and joyfully give to someone else. If you have a witness in your heart to share something you have with someone, you should not ignore or shut out God's voice, but obey. That is the kind thing to do.

How to recognize a greedy person

A greedy person brings trouble to his family. As seen in Proverbs 15:27, it cannot be disputed that,

"A greedy person brings trouble to his family." (ICB)

How does he do that? Well, one example of this is if you make purchases and commit your family to debt, you are bringing trouble to your family. You run the risk of causing your family to experience troubling things such as eviction notices; letters from collectors; re-possession of vehicles, and so on...all distressing and troublesome things!

Greed creates confusion and strife.

A greedy man stirs up division wherever he is: maybe in a family, church, or even the community. Proverbs 28:25 teaches,

"The greedy person stirs up dissension, but the one who trusts in the Lord will prosper." (NET)

The greedy person lays claim to that which is not his and stirs up contentions and arguments. Such people are in a rush to get rich and refuse to allow for the process of work and investing to produce their just reward. As such, they

make terrible financial judgements and end up in all kinds of confusion. They blame others for their bad choices. Greedy people borrow and do not pay back. These things divide friends and families. Be careful about lending a greedy person money, cars, or anything precious that you do not want to lose. You may never see it again!

When you strive for success, strive lawfully.

Greed is a bad attitude amongst people; it is resentful and antagonistic in nature. Instead of resorting to conflicts and aggressive behavior when you strive for success, I would advise that you strive lawfully. Do not carry news on co-workers and friends to get ahead; you do not have to put other people down to make progress in life. In speaking about this, I heard an old wise preacher say this, *"Why does it have to be me **or** you? Why can't it be you **and** me? We can do this thing **together!**"* We can live together, we can prosper together, and we can get the blessing together. If you get a big house, there is always room in the world for a bigger house. You cannot be intimated by the success and blessing of others. If you do, you are denying yourself the right to come into abundance.

A greedy person is also an unjust person. If you are unjust and unfair to people, you will not prosper nor be stable. Look at Proverbs 29:4,

> *"By justice a king gives a country stability, but those who are greedy for bribes tear it down."* (NIV)

That means, where there is unfairness and the ill-treatment of people, that family, ministry, or nation is going to fall. When you live with a certain degree of unfairness, you cannot be stable.

Greed and the unfair treatment of other people will bounce back in your life.

Whilst justice brings stability and joy in a person's life, greed destroys it. So much so, that at any point anything that they build can fall.

A greedy person is prone to stealing! When a greedy person has a craving for something and cannot get it, stealing is bound to happen. But, unjust people will free the guilty and slaughter the innocent. They do **whatever** it takes to get what they want.

A greedy person eats excessively. In the world of eating, greed is called *"gluttony."* Some people are never satisfied when it comes to food, and resort to over-eating or gluttonous behavior.

In the scriptures, there are over forty categories of people that we are warned to be careful with. In 1 Corinthians 5:9-11 some of these are listed, and the 'greedy person' is among the number. Let's look at what it says:

> *"⁹ I wrote to you in my letter not to associate with sexually immoral people—*
>
> *¹⁰not at all meaning the people of this world who are immoral, or the greedy and swindlers, or idolaters. In that case you would have to leave this world. ¹¹But now I am writing to you that you must not associate with anyone who claims to be a brother or sister but is sexually immoral or greedy, an idolater or slanderer, a drunkard or swindler. Do not even eat with such people."*

This is not talking about unsaved people, because if that were so, we would have to leave the world. Paul is cautioning us not to associate with 'a brother' who is greedy, and with idolaters, swindlers, or drunks; do not eat with them. If you want to walk in prosperity, be careful with greedy people.

Greedy people do not enjoy serving others. In 1 Peter chapter 5 verse 2, Paul warns the local Shepherd not to be greedy for dishonest gain, but to be willing to serve.

"² Be shepherds of God's flock that is under your care, watching over them—not because you must, but because you are willing, as God wants you to be; not pursuing dishonest gain, but eager to serve."

When people serve, they should be adequately rewarded, but it must be motivated out of a heart that is clean and pure. To be a good servant you must learn how to humble yourself; it does not matter how prestigious the position is. There is greatness in serving, but greedy people think that they are the only ones who are worthy of service and honor.

Humility is the ability to ignore your own importance!

There are some other characteristics that are associated with greed, such as 'ungratefulness', 'boasting', and 'being a lover of your own self'. All of these traits belong to the same family of sin as 'greed' and are sure to block up the blessings in your life.

186

How to solve the issue of greed

- Recognize that you have a problem. To deny its existence delays your ability to solve the problem and to unlock the power of God. If you get rid of it from your heart, a simple prayer could unlock a huge miracle in your life.

- You must admit that there is a problem and repent. Tell God that you found difficulty in serving other people because there was greed in your heart.

- Look for someone that you know is getting ahead in life and commend them. Practice commending and praising other people. Bless the sister for a good song, bless the preacher for a good word, bless the brother for a good exhortation, commend the musicians and tell them that they blessed you, commend the sister and tell her that she looks great in her dress. Practice commending and praising other people. That way, you are destroying the power of greed at work in your heart. After you have repented of your sin, start acting differently and the power of God will be released in your life.

- Finally, trust God for your breakthrough, depend on God for your blessing, and don't look on the things of another and wish that they didn't have it and you did. The same God

who blessed them, can bless you too. The color of your skin and your educational background does not determine God's love for you. Trust in the Lord and do not rely on your own understanding. He will bring wonderful things to pass in your life, and He will provide all your needs according to His riches in glory by Christ Jesus.

CONCLUSION

I t is very clear that any economy—be it personal or national—should be built upon a strong moral foundation. A moral foundation is the strength of any people. Indeed, righteousness exalts a nation, but sin brings disgrace to any people.

But it should be noted that God does not want us to avoid the previously discussed iniquitous habits purely on the basis of wanting things from His hands. He desires that we refrain from such behavior as an act of love towards Him and because of a deep yearning in our hearts to live righteously before a holy God. Therefore, any discovered sinful behavior in our lives must be altered; and irreproachable habits be established permanently in its place. Righteousness is a powerful force. When we walk in integrity, we walk in power and in security.

It is important for us to remember that bad habits of every kind do not just have the *potential* to prevent the free flow of blessings from getting to us, but they *actually* create an impenetrable barricade that is resistant to these blessings. Bad habits shut the windows of Heaven from responding favorably to us, hence, the loving reproof of *"DO NOT serve other gods; DO NOT commit adultery; DO NOT lie, steal, covet and so on..."* that is enveloped in the 'Ten Commandments'.

It is the benevolence of our Lord that prompts Him to issue these commands to safeguard us from the adverse effects of iniquitous behavior. His perfect will is to lavish us with blessings in great abundance but cannot do so when sin has erected a reprehensible wall that impedes these blessings.

As we honestly search our hearts for any sign of iniquity, and sincerely repent before our merciful God, obstacles that have been hindering our blessings shall be forcefully blasted away by the stroke of God's favor!!! It will give way to the abundant supply of God's kingdom, of which He takes great pleasure in lavishly pouring upon His children.

> *"³² Fear not, little flock; for* **it is your Father's good pleasure to give you the kingdom!**" (Luke 12:32 – KJV)

NOTES

Law of attraction
Experience is not the greatest
teacher. following instruction
is the greatest teacher
Satan will never be divided against
himself, he's a poking demon, he
will not move from his assignment

NOTES

NOTES

NOTES

NOTES

_____

_____

_____

_____

_____

_____

_____

_____

_____

_____

_____

_____

_____

_____

_____

_____

_____

_____

_____

_____

_____

_____

_____

_____

_____

_____

_____

NOTES

More Great Resources From Dr. Peter Bonadie Ministries

Books:
- Understanding The Kingdom
- Curses, Causes and Cures
- Seven Manifestations of the Curse
- You Can Make Dry Bones Live
- Kingdom of gods
- Altars to Thrones
- Undesirables

Contact Information:

DR. PETER BONADIE MINISTRIES
770 Park Place
Brooklyn, New York 11216
Phone: 1.888.643.4442
Email: apostlebonadie@gmail.com
www.peterbonadieministries.org